In Search of Truth ...

An Analytical Approach to the Interview Process

DANIEL T. MARSANO, CIFI, CFE

Artwork by Jane Stroschin

Henry Quill Press
Fremont, Michigan

ISBN 1-883960-22-3

Production services provided by Hermitage Publishing Services,
1858 Pleasantville Road, Suite 159, Briarcliff Manor, New York
10510

Designed by Harry Nolan

Artwork by Jane Stroschin

Manufacturing services provided Imago Sales USA

Printed in Hong Kong

10 9 8 7 6 5 4 3 2 1

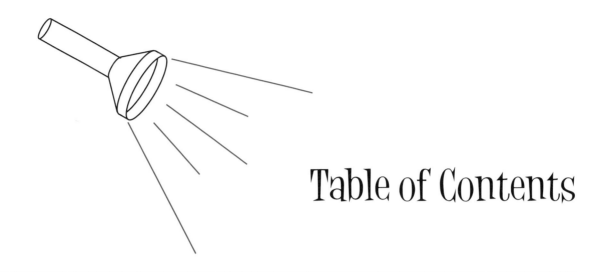

Table of Contents

PART 3: Detailing the Inquiry

PART 4: Detection of Deception During the Detailed Inquiry

PART 5: Closing the Interview

For Edward P. Hels

For bestowing your wisdom, your guidance,
and your vision

For V. James Meola

For believing and providing the support
and opportunity for professional growth

For Stanley Ball

For your unwavering faith, confidence,
and most of all, your trust

In the Beginning......................there was the "Old School!"

It was hot! The Old Light Guard Armory on 8 Mile Road had been there, it seemed, for a millennium. Air conditioning certainly did not exist when it was built and it was obvious that no one seemed to deem it important enough to add. Seated at my table in the large room, I began to look for signs of a breeze coming through the open crank windows that lined the southern wall. There weren't any.

It was the Summer of 1972. I was a rookie police officer in the middle of my training at the Metropolitan Police Academy. It would last ten weeks. The room was full of other rookies from various police departments around southeastern Michigan, most of whom I did not know. There were about a hundred of us, lined up three to a table classroom style, and silently, on that sweltering afternoon, we all listened to the lecture.

The topic was Police Courtesy. For six hours, a Police Captain from Port Huron Police Department droned on. He drew pictures on the chalkboard depicting a garden. Then he told us how to plant that garden. He said, "Let's plant three rows of Ps; Promptness, Preparedness, and Politeness! We'll also need two rows of Squash; Squash Criticism, Squash Complaints!" And so he went, on and on and on! It was incredible!

That afternoon stands out so strongly in my mind as a result of the sharp contrast to how the day had begun. We had started that morning's instruction with a two hour class on Interviewing and Interrogation Techniques. I had found the topic fascinating and was totally focused on the Detroit Police Homicide Detective as he described various questioning tactics and how they had evolved over the years. I had wondered how the time had gone by so fast in all that heat and why only two hours had been allotted to this topic. I craved more information. But it was not to be. Police Courtesy took over the rest of the day and I received only one more hour of training in Interviewing and Interrogation Techniques during that entire ten weeks.

As I reflect upon that time, I am still amazed. The most important skill that a police officer needs to be effective in his work is the ability to conduct an interview. How was it possible that my training as a rookie police officer could be so devoid of such instruction? Surely, I reasoned, when I began my full time work with a seasoned training officer in the field, this would be rectified. But, it was not to be.

Upon completion of the Police Academy, I was assigned to the Uniform Division, Road Patrol. I rode with a senior officer for the first four months and then was put out on my own in a one-man car. Formal instruction was over and from then on, what I did, and how I learned to do it, was strictly left up to me.

Two and a half years later, at the ripe old age of twenty-three, I was promoted to Detective. I arrived for my first day on the job dressed in a yellow leisure suit and brown patent leather shoes. I was young, excited, and thoroughly unprepared for my new responsibilities. Immediately upon my arrival that day, I was given my first assignment. A suspect, in a Robbery-Armed case, was in custody. My Sergeant instructed me to begin an interrogation. I had, I told him, only limited experience in doing interrogations. I was sure that there must be a special technique that the detectives employed to conduct these sessions. So, not wanting to make a mistake in my first attempt, I asked for some guidance in this endeavor.

A senior detective was then appointed to take me through the ropes. Now, I determined, I would learn the real techniques! But, it was not to be. As we were about to enter the interview room, the other detective stopped me, put his hand on my shoulder, and gave me this sage advice. "Listen," he said. "If you want to do a successful interrogation you have to be able to ask a lot of questions. Now, pay attention, watch what I do, and do yours the same way in the future."

We spent close to two hours in the interview room that morning. The senior detective asked question after question. He was doggedly persis-

tent and extremely tenacious in his approach. The suspect was cringing in fear, sweating profusely, and looked, for all the world, like a guilty person. Or perhaps, he just looked like a scared innocent person. In either case he was certainly scared. But for all the bluster, fire, and brimstone, there would be no confession that day.

For my next few interrogation situations, I attempted to pattern myself after this approach. I did not do very well at it and it never seemed to fit me. I was extremely uncomfortable and I didn't understand why. I questioned whether or not I was cut out for this type of work. If I was incapable of obtaining confessions, what good was I as a detective? So, I went back to my senior detective instructor and asked him how he had learned his methods. When he told me, I was dumb struck!

He had been taught by a senior officer some fifteen years before. That officer had learned from another senior officer fifteen years before that, and so on. Then, standing more erect, head back, stomach sucked in, he proudly stated, "I'm from the 'Old School'! My skills have been passed down from generation to generation!"

"So," I said. "Then, if I'm to understand you correctly, you are doing things the way they were done circa 1930?"

I do not recall what, if anything, he said in response to my question. I think the magnitude of this revelation was entirely lost upon him. Could he not hear what it was that he was really saying? Had we really learned nothing new since 1930? Were those old ways that grew out of the dark rooms with the dangling light bulbs still the best? Had we not learned anything more about human nature and behavior in all those years?

As I pondered this more and more, I grew troubled inside. I was convinced that there had to be a better approach to interviewing and interrogation than what we were doing. I knew that something was very wrong with our method and there had to be a better way. I didn't know what that way was though, and worse yet, I didn't even know how to find out!

That was the crossroads point in my professional career. I had to make a decision to accept those things that were, or to go in search of something better. It was clear that I would never be successful conducting an interview or an interrogation by continuing to employ methods that I did not believe in. I would have to learn more, and I would have to do it on my own.

Since that time, I have taken classes, read books, watched videos, attended lectures and seminars across the country, and sought the knowledge of all I could find. My desire to discover more and more became something of an obsession. I studied non-verbal behavior, kinesics, neuro-linguistics, and statement analysis. I tried new ideas and worked out solutions to old problems. I learned to categorize types of interviews and the importance in recognizing the differences between an interview and an interrogation. I found that statement analysis techniques could be used effectively during the interviewing process and I adapted them accordingly. I recognized the danger that exists when my emotions enter the processes and how to incorporate strategies instead.

Knowledge led to increased confidence, and together, they led to new successes. Interviews and interrogations became challenging and exciting. I found myself continually buoyed by the surprises that I would encounter with each new interview and each new interrogation. I couldn't help but be amazed by the things that people would tell me. And I was stupefied by the things that people would admit to. How could it be that one could entice such behavior from another person? Was the human mind so fragile that it could be manipulated so easily? Or, was it simply a matter of tactics?

Whatever the reason, one thing was definitely certain. I was becoming incredibly successful and it wasn't due to any innate knowledge that I brought with me from the womb. Indeed, I had become little more than an information conglomerate, combining the best methods that I had found from many, many sources into my own system. But it only became possible when I made the decision to leave behind forever.........the "Old School!"

PART 1

The Interview

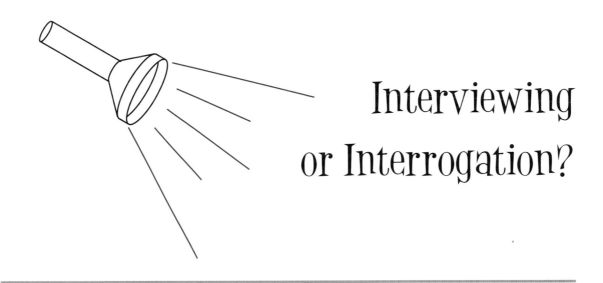

CHAPTER 1

Interviewing or Interrogation?

Interviewing and Interrogation are spoken together so often that one would almost assume that they are both parts of the same process. This couldn't be further from the truth. There are actually three different forms of interviewing, all of which differ greatly from an interrogation. Though they are all related in that they have some forms of commonality, many differences remain, and success in any of these procedures depends on the acceptance and understanding of that fact.

3 FORMS OF INTERVIEWING

What exactly is an interview?

Interview Defined: An Interview is a discussion about a specific subject that is best conducted between two persons, where the purpose for the interviewer is to explore the subject matter and to gather accurate information.

This definition covers a great deal of ground. Almost any conversation between any two persons would qualify itself as an interview. Therefore, it is the purpose of the interview that is the determining characteristic which dictates the approach and format that the interviewer must use in order to become successful.

An investigator, who is out talking to witnesses to a fire, has one objective in mind. He wants to obtain as much information as possible to assist him in uncovering how the fire started, who may have been responsible for it, who may benefit by it, etc. His purpose is very clearly – **Information Gathering.**

In another instance, an investigator may be faced with an employee theft situation involving ten possible suspects. His intent in conducting interviews here is to assess probable guilt or innocence. Since the purpose of these interviews is vastly different from Information Gathering, they require different tactics. This form of interviewing is called – **Suspect Elimination.**

An employer seeking to hire someone to fill a sensitive position would be very concerned about the honesty and integrity of the prospective employee. His purpose in an interview with the person is to determine whether or not he possesses the type of moral character necessary for the position. To accomplish this, the employer would conduct an – **Integrity Interview.**

INTERROGATION

Interrogation Defined: An Interrogation differs from an interview in that it is a controlled conversation between two persons with the purpose being to go beyond the accumulation of facts to the obtaining of a confession or an admission from a guilty person.

An interrogation, therefore, is a different communication process altogether. While not an interview at all, it can grow out of an interview when the investigator senses that he is on the right track. In that event, the investigator may move from an interviewing mode into an interrogation mode. But at that point, what is transpiring between the investigator and the subject, ceases to be an interview.

All three forms of interviewing are important aspects of knowledge for a successful investigator to master. Far and away the most common amongst them is the Information Gathering Interview. This type of interview takes place between persons in all parts of daily life. Every conversation between two people that has any single subject focus will qualify itself as an Information Gathering Interview. We all participate in this process during our normal interactions with other people. The investigator needs to be especially skilled in this area, though, as his very job function is dependent upon it. Understanding that, every facet of the process needs to be examined to assure that we are obtaining the maximum amount of information available while still making sound judgments about its accuracy.

It is the Information Gathering Interview which this book will address, covering methods for increasing the amount of information that is obtained. But just as importantly, we must utilize techniques to detect when information is being withheld and/or when deception is present. It is not enough to sense that something is wrong with what we are hearing. We must also be consciously aware of WHY we are sensing it. Linguistic techniques help us to identify deception and they give us the means to defeat it.

CHAPTER II

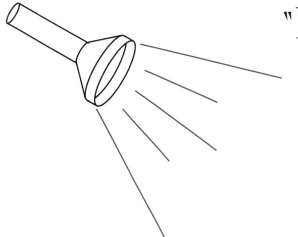

"Everyone wants to give every information to everyone!"

- Avinoam Sapir

I first heard those words while attending a seminar on Scientific Content Analysis. The lecturer, Avinoam Sapir, is one of the modern founders of Statement Analysis, a process of examining the content of written statements and transcripts by looking at the words people choose. Mr. Sapir was merely expressing a phenomenon that is incredibly evident, yet seldom noticed.

People like to talk! They will tell you virtually anything! All we have to do, as interviewers, is remove obstacles that prevent this natural occurrence. We don't have to find ways to get people to talk. We need only enable them to do so by making it easier for them. I don't know why we, as human beings, seem to have this insatiable need to impart information to others. But the fact is that we do! So, to succeed as an interviewer, one must first embrace this truth.

Have you ever been on an airplane? Have you ever noticed how two complete strangers will strike up a conversation when seated next to each other for a long flight? Listen sometime to what they tell each other. They will discuss their families, marital problems, past drug usage, job difficulties, etc. They will reveal intimate details of their lives to someone they have known for less than an hour and whose name they may never know!

I was in Cancun a couple of years ago with my family and friends. We were staying at a very nice hotel with a beautiful pool. I went to the towel booth to get towels for all of us, eight in total. At the booth the young woman had to find the stitched-in numbers on the towels and record them with my name and room number to assure that I would not steal them. Probably of more importance, though, while she was doing that, they had me as a captive audience to the man in the adjoining booth who was selling excursions. He wanted to sell our group a scuba diving adventure, boat rides, underwater submarine observation, jet skiing, hang gliding, and more. While the young woman laboriously executed her task, in nearly slow motion, I was a victim of the motor-mouthed pitch man.

As the man talked, I noticed what appeared to me, to be a Canadian accent. I'm quite familiar with it since I reside in the Detroit area, just across the river from Windsor, Ontario. We frequently travel to Canada and often meet and speak with Canadians visiting Michigan. Seeking to derail his sales presentation, I asked the man about his accent.

He smiled broadly and said, "I'm from Vancouver! I bought a one-way ticket and I'm never going back. I've been her 352 days now!"

"That's marvelous," I replied. "You must really like it here."

"Sure do," he said. "In my first two weeks here, I had a job, a girlfriend, and an apartment. And now, I've still got the same job and the same girlfriend, and I've just changed apartments."

"What do you like about it here?" I asked.

"Just look around you," he said. "Look at the beautiful beaches, the beautiful weather, the gorgeous women! How could you not like that?" And then, he lowered his voice, looked side to side, and spoke again, as if these gestures somehow created great privacy. "Of course I really don't like to use condoms," he said. "So I figured I better find a girlfriend right away. We've been together now for almost a year and I have really grown to like her!"

"How really GRAND for her!" I replied.

What just happened here? I only wanted towels. But I ended up talking to a transplanted Canadian who wanted to tell me about his sex life! Why? What made him so eager to reveal personal information in this way? Wasn't that strange?

No, it was just human nature at work. It was a prime example of the principle rule that one must adhere to if one wants to obtain information. People like to talk, and they will tell you virtually anything!

At a suburban Chicago hotel, I was seated in a restaurant one evening having coffee with Linda, an investigator with whom I work. I was there attending a week long seminar on a new form of interviewing and interrogation techniques. She was working a couple of cases in the area and staying in the same hotel. We were discussing the propensity that people have to talk and she was expressing some doubts about the limits of this theory.

I suggested that we try the waitress who was approaching the table. Linda agreed, and when the young woman arrived to inquire if we wanted anything else, I asked her, "Have you been working here long?"

"No," she replied. "I've only been working here for a couple of days. I haven't always been a waitress. In fact, don't tell the management, but this is my very first waitress job. They thought that I had experience. Actually, I'm a travel agent, but the company that I was working for went out of business, so I had to start working here."

"Why not another travel agency," I inquired.

"Well," she said, "that's exactly what I'm going to do as soon as I can find another position. This work isn't so bad, but it doesn't pay all that well and, after all, I am divorced with three kids to feed! They're 12, 9, and 8 years old, and their father doesn't contribute a thing! I have to do it all myself! He's a real asshole!"

"I see," I said. "I'm from Detroit, and Linda here is from Indianapolis. We're just in town for a couple of days on business."

"That's great," she said. "I hope you enjoy your stay here. If you need anything else, just let me know."

With that, she abruptly walked away from our table. Why? What had happened to cause her to quit talking? Why was she so open about herself when first prompted, and then so quick to exit the conversation?

Simply put, I had moved the spotlight. People love to talk about themselves. They aren't all that interested in hearing about others. So, when I took the focus of the conversation off of the waitress, she lost interest in continuing it. She didn't want to hear about me or where I was from. She didn't care about Linda or where she was from. She was only tuned in to herself.

Move the spotlight — lose information! This is another cardinal rule of human behavior that one must learn to accept if one is to become a successful interviewer. So, if people want to talk, and they want to talk about themselves, how do we maximize our gain from knowing this? That part is easy. We simply ask questions.

People are not afraid to answer questions. They are only afraid to ask them. How many times have you failed to ask someone a question because you thought they wouldn't answer it? How many times have you not sought information because you had already decided that the person would not tell you? "I'm not going to call him and ask that!" you said. "He'd never tell me!" How do you know? Why do we, as human beings, automatically say, "No!", for the other person? What is it that causes such fear?

In a word, it is REJECTION! We all fear REJECTION. And asking a question that someone does not, or will not, answer is a form of rejection. So, we hesitate, and avoid asking the tough question, dealing with the tough people, and being too inquisitive with anyone. We don't want to be told, "No!" And when someone refuses to tell us what we ask, that person is, in effect, telling us, "No!"

Ah, but I've learned something more about this word, "No!". The bank of negative responses within a human being is really quite limited. People have trouble saying, "No!". In fact, it is statistically true that 97% of people will answer a question the second time that it is asked. So, we need only repeat our question to the person who has refused an answer and we already have a 97% likelihood that we will get the answer the second time around. If we don't, then we just ask it a third time.

All of this results in two hard and fast principles about interviewing that we must come to terms with and accept. People want to talk and they want to talk about themselves. What is important is WHAT we ask and HOW we ask it. That is the key to success in an **Information Gathering Interview.**

CHAPTER III

Elements of
the Interview

There are five steps necessary for a successful **Information Gathering Interview.**

1. **Preparation:** Determining the Purpose and Objective of the Interview

2. **Opening:** Establishment of Authority and Development of Rapport

3. **Listening:** Allowing the Person to Talk – NO Interruptions!

4. **Specific Questions:** Detailing the Information Developed

5. Closing: Summary – Repeat of Important Assertions – Open for Re-
contact

Having first prepared for the interview, what considerations should be
given to the opening itself? **Attitude** is the first thing that comes to
mind. Since we want the subject to talk to us, we must exhibit an expectation for him to talk and we must enable him to do so by every action and
word we use. This makes the interviewer's attitude rather critical. We
want to present ourselves as a model listener to the subject. What quali-
ties should we show?

1. Objective

2. Even Tempered

3. Sincere

4. Interested

5. Polite

6. Understanding

Our **Tone of Voice** when talking to the subject is important as well.
What would be the ideal?

1. Medium, Conversational

2. No Skepticism

3. Smooth Speech

Note: A point to note here is that a low, quiet, conversational tone
demonstrates privacy. If the subject is talking about a sensitive area that
he feels very private about, the interviewer should lower his voice, speak-

ing quietly and softly. This gives the aura of increased privacy and makes the subject feel more comfortable and at ease as he talks.

Another consideration is a concept called **Modeling.** This is a capitalization on the fact that people respond best to others who are like themselves. How do we do this?

1. Voice Tone

2. Pace of Speech

3. Language

A person who speaks with very poor grammar and talks softly, at a very slow pace, does all of these things for a reason. The poor grammar is a product of his environment and educational background. The softness of the speech could be related to mood, emotions, or any number of other factors. The slow pace of speech is an indication of how fast the subject mentally processes information.

So what would happen if the interviewer began asking questions of this subject in collegiate English, in a loud voice, and at a rapid pace? Quite simply, the interviewer will develop no rapport and lose the subject's attention. That will further result in loss of information. This will happen because the subject will be unable to identify with the language, intimidated by the volume of the speech, and lost by the pace of the words. If the subject doesn't understand the words and is bothered by the volume, it will be difficult for him to relax and dispense information. The pace of the speech can be very critical as well because the subject may not be able to process the words that quickly.

This is why we work to model the subject. The use of this technique greatly enhances the interviewer's rapport with the subject and increases dramatically the amount of information that can be obtained.

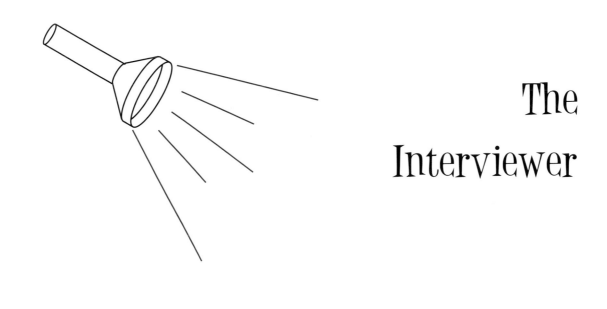

CHAPTER IV

The Interviewer

Anyone who seeks information from another person is, in effect, an interviewer. This can be any person from any walk of life. This can be someone performing in an occupational capacity such as a teacher talking to a parent to learn more about a child in class, or a butcher trying to determine what cut of meat the customer needs. It can be a homeowner seeking information about a city road project from a neighbor or a young girl getting batting tips from her softball coach. It can be a shopper seeking bargains from a retailer or a barber collecting local gossip from his patrons. Everyone is an interviewer and everyone is an interviewing subject at any given time.

Some people conduct interviews as their primary job function. This immediately brings us to think of the professional investigator, but there are a host of other positions where interviewing is the main ingredient of their work. Consider, for example, an employment counselor, a stock broker, a newspaper reporter, an attorney, an accountant, a census taker, a salesperson, etc. Many are the jobs that require interviewing skills as the most important ingredient.

To the investigator, however, the stakes are somewhat different. The subject of his interview may have much more at risk than someone being asked by a salesperson what type of suit he would like. The interview is seen as an event in and of itself. This necessitates that the interviewer give thought to where, when, and how the interview will take place, as well as who should be present.

All interviews and interrogations should take place one on one. An additional person in the room will never work to the advantage of the interviewer and thus can only serve to hinder the process. If there is a specific reason for the presence of another person, the interviewer must take every step possible to limit the distraction. The second person should be seated off to the side, out of the normal sight line of the subject. That person must not speak at any time, take notes, or physically do anything which will call attention to himself. As much as possible, the subject's words and actions need to be totally responsive to the stimulus provided by the interviewer, not the second person. This allows the interviewer to remain in full control of the interview and to make more accurate judgments about what he is hearing and seeing.

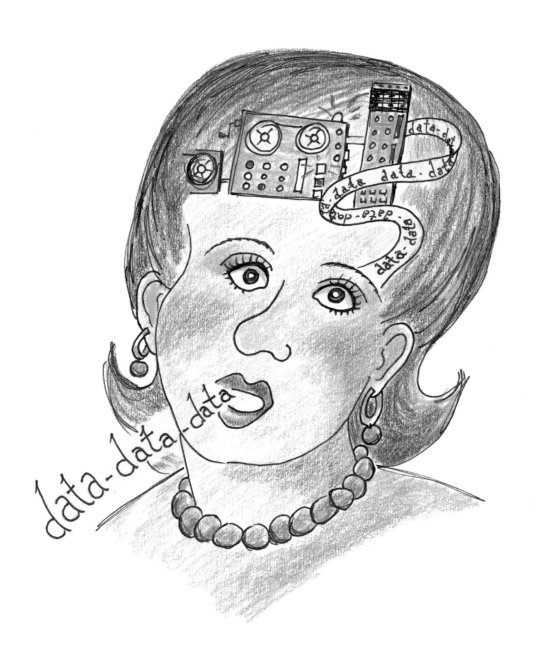

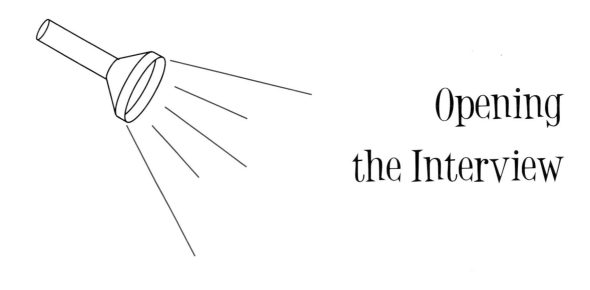

CHAPTER V

Opening
the Interview

How the interview is opened is every bit as important as how it is concluded. Setting the subject up, establishing authority, and creating structural control are vital to success. The interviewer accomplishes this through the use of **Personal Data Questions.**

The interviewer will ask the subject his name, address, phone number, Social Security number, etc. If he already has this information, he may just go over it with the subject, ostensibly to verify the accuracy of what he has in his file.

Interviewer: "Mr. Jones, I see that you live at 123 Oak Street, is that correct?"

Subject: "Yes, that's right."

Interviewer: "And that's in Anytown, is that correct?"

Subject: "Yeah."

Interviewer: "And, I have your phone number here as, 555-2345, would that be right?"

Subject: "Yeah."

Interviewer: "Okay, and what is your Social Security number?"

Subject: "That's 123-45-6789."

What just happened during this exchange? Did the interviewer really learn any new or valuable information from the subject? No, he did not. What he did do, though, is three things:

1. Established of a structure of ? - . - ? - . - ? - . - ? - .

2. Brought about the subject's psychological acceptance of the interviewer's authority to ask questions.

3. Created the subject's psychological acceptance of his responsibility to answer the questions.

Everything spoken by the interviewer ended in a question mark and everything spoken by the subject ended in a period. This structure of question mark followed by period puts the interviewer firmly in control of the interview. Further, the repetition of the pattern brings the subject to accept the interviewer's authority to ask him questions as well as his own responsibility to answer them. It is vital that these things be established very early in the process, as they will dictate the course of the interview. The interviewer must then endeavor to maintain this structure throughout the interview.

CHAPTER VI

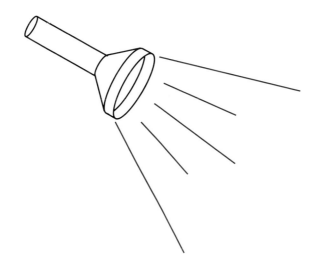

Obtaining the Pure Version of the Story

Once the interviewer has taken control of the interview and established authority, it is time to extract maximum information from the subject. This is best accomplished by reaching for the subject's pure, unblemished account of what he knows. The interviewer does not want this to be tainted by specific questions. This is the point at which the time sharing between the interviewer and the subject should be clearly fixed at:

Interviewer: 5 % -   **Subject:** 95 %

For many investigators, this is a radically new approach. We are taught as we prepare for each interview to concentrate on getting answers to the questions which originally led us to talk with the subject. We may have

written lists of questions. We may just keep them all in our minds. But, we DO have questions. Our first instinct is to begin firing away with those questions at the first possible opportunity.

There is a problem with this approach. **Specific Questions** do two things:

1. Teach the subject what is important to us.

2. Teach the subject how to lie to us.

It has further been established that information which comes as an answer to a **Specific Question** is less reliable than information that comes without a question. So why would we want to open an interview with a list of questions? We can always ask specific questions later in the interview. Don't we have an opportunity to learn far more by letting the subject speak first? More likely than not, the subject will answer most of our questions while telling his story. Additionally, we will learn a great deal of other information that we didn't even know to ask about and, perhaps more importantly, we will have the opportunity to analyze the story without first contaminating it with our focus and our questions.

Therefore, the interviewer needs to listen to the subject's story completely and thoroughly before beginning to ask any questions of his own. This is accomplished by asking **Open and Generalized Questions.** These are:

1. Questions which encourage the subject to go into a narration.

2. Questions which cannot be answered with a "Yes" or a "No".

The objective of these questions is to induce the subject talk and continue talking. The interviewer wants this to occur without any guidance as to what to say or how to say it. The subject has a story and the interviewer must simply remove all roadblocks to enable the subject to tell it. For the interviewer, this is only one interview in hundreds and hundreds. For the subject, however, this is the ONLY interview and the subject WILL have a story to tell.

Note: An oral recitation of a story is not a chronology or a reality. It is only what the person has decided to tell us.

During this part of the interview, there must be **No Interruptions!** Any interruption will cause the subject to break from the flow of his story and could cost the interviewer critical information. Even if the interviewer is confused about a specific aspect of the story, or a name that the subject used, there must be no interruptions. We can always ask questions later, but at this juncture, the interviewer MUST listen.

This narration may be helped along by the interviewer's encouragement to continue. We accomplish this by letting the subject know that we are listening. Short Expressions of Interest are useful here:

1. Shock – Words like, "Wow!", or, "Really?"

2. Sympathy – Phrases like, "I'm sorry!", or, "That's awful!"

3. Amusement – Smiling or chuckling outwardly.

4. Empathy – Phrases like, "That must have been very difficult!", or, "It must be very painful!"

All of these are methods by which we encourage the subject to tell us his story. They give us material to work with to detect deception while we are maximizing the amount of information that we are obtaining.

Will this add to the length of time spent during an interview? Yes, it will. But an interviewer will make one of two mistakes every time he conducts

an interview. It is unavoidable. If the interviewer follows all of the paths to maximize the information gained, he will certainly have to sift through a great deal of unnecessary garbage to do so. But if the interviewer attempts to shorten the interview to save time, he will lose information as a veritable certainty. The interviewer must, therefore, either lose time or lose information. There is no way to avoid doing one or the other. Losing time can be a problem, but losing information is intolerable!

CHAPTER VII

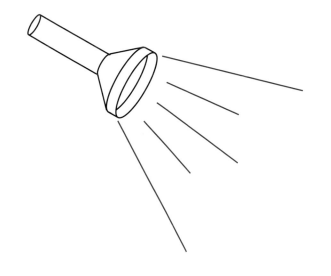

Listening to the Story

There are two ways to listen to people:

1. The interviewer may listen to the sequence of events as related.

2. The interviewer may listen to the language the subject uses.

The first is a natural behavior and is the way that we all listen. We tune in to the events as the subject relates them and we follow along as the story develops. We become interested in facts and occurrences and make mental notes of times, dates, people, and places. When we are concerned with detecting deception we begin to inspect the facts and look for discrepancies. But that is not the only place to look.

The second way to listen to someone is to listen to the language used. This is not a natural tendency. We are so concerned with facts that we don't hear the words. It is the subject's language, however, upon which the interviewer must fully concentrate in order to pick up the information hidden in his word choices. It is there that the interviewer will find the true clues to deception and/or missing information.

How do we begin to listen to the language in a story? We start by remaining cognizant of three very important points. We will refer to them as the **3 Golden Principles.**

1. The Story MUST Remain in First Person, Singular, Past Tense!

As a person relates a story to us of something which has happened, it is very clearly rooted in the past. The past does not take place in the present. Therefore, the verb tense must certainly be past tense as well. Further, the person telling the story is relating first hand information. Thus the story should be expressed in the first person, singular. Any deviation from this formula should cause the interviewer to be concerned about the accuracy of what is being related.

2. No Coincidence! Every Word the Person Says Has a Meaning!

As a person is relating a story we want to believe what he is saying. Human nature will cause us to extend extra latitude to him, often overlooking words or dismissing them as just a mistake or a slip of the tongue. We say to ourselves, "He didn't really mean to say that!" We then give him the benefit of the doubt and skip past whatever we have just noticed. An interviewer must be very careful of this pitfall. In ALL circumstances, EVERY word has a meaning and must not be ignored!

3. Until a Subject Says that Something Happened, It Didn't Happen!

This is the most difficult concept of the **3 Golden Principles.** Simply put, all this means is that we must not read additional meaning into what a person tells us beyond the very literal sense of what was said. We cannot assume anything more than precisely what is conveyed by the subject's words.

These three principles will be covered further as we venture on to detect deception in later chapters. They are the three points that the interviewer must continually remind himself to listen for as a subject tells his story.

CHAPTER VIII

Note Taking

Investigators are notorious note takers. We are taught to be very precise in recording facts and we always endeavor to be exact. Naturally, this causes the investigator to be very judicious in his note taking to ensure accuracy when later recounting what has transpired in his written report. What the investigator does not always consider is the damage that can be caused by note taking during an **Information Gathering Interview,** if done at the wrong time.

There are times to take notes and there are times not to. Certainly, as the interview is opened and the interviewer is asking the Personal Data questions, it would be expected that he take notes. The subject would be concerned if he did not take notes at this point. However, upon the completion of that part of the process, it is imperative that the interviewer close the note pad, set the pen down and turn his full attention to the subject.

As the interviewer obtains the **Pure Version of the Story,** he must be totally focused on every word the subject is saying. He cannot do that while writing notes. He will miss additional information even as he is diligently working to remember other information. The negative consequences of note taking during this portion of the interview greatly outweigh any benefits.

Just as Specific Questions aid the subject, **Note Taking** will:

1. Tell the subject what the focus is and what is important to the interviewer.

2. Teaches the subject how to lie.

When a subject is relating a story and the interviewer suddenly begins to write, it causes the subject to pause. He is distracted from what he was about to say and he begins to consider what he already DID say that caused the interviewer to start taking notes. He starts to wonder what the interviewer found to be important about what he had just said. This interrupts the flow of the story and the interviewer loses a great deal of information as a result. As the interview continues, the subject begins to understand the focus of the interview better and better. This teaches the subject how to lie to the interviewer and how to manipulate the information that he is giving. All of this very adversely affects both the amount of information obtained and the ability to make judgments about its accuracy.

Later in the interview, as we begin to ask specific questions which expand upon the information obtained here, note taking will be permissible. Even at that time, though, it should be kept to a minimum. Note taking is now, and forever will be, a greater hindrance than a help during this type of interview process.

The pros and cons of the use of tape recorders during the **Information Gathering Interview** have been debated for many years. While I accept that they are necessary in some forms of investigative interviews, such as the Recorded Statement taken in property and casualty insurance claim losses, I am opposed to them at any other time. It its purest sense, the interview must focus first, and foremost, upon obtaining maximum information and detecting deception. Anything presenting an obstacle to that must be eliminated. The tape recorder creates an obstacle because it increases the subject's anxiety and inhibits the natural flow of information. Causing the subject to be guarded leads to an alteration in the language that the subject uses and reduces the advantages of analyzing those words to detect missing information and/or deception.

This does not mean that the use of a tape recorder will render linguistic analysis useless, but it will somewhat reduce the amount of clues available to the interviewer, and that is unacceptable. While there are ways to minimize the effect of the presence of a tape recorder, the interviewer must look for every advantage available to him. A tape recorder is not conducive to this goal and thus should never be used when not necessary.

PART 2

Detection of Deception During the Interview

CHAPTER IX

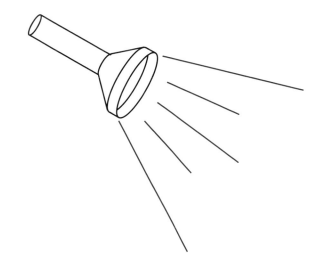

Analysis: Verbal vs Non-Verbal

NON-VERBAL BEHAVIOR ANALYSIS

Non-verbal behavior analysis is a very valid scientific process. The trained interviewer can make many exceptionally good judgments about truth or deception during an interview with the use of this technique. It does have its limitations, however. Non-verbal behavior may be affected by a large number of outside stimuli. An interview taking place in a pristine, clean, uncluttered interview room without windows or other distractions, would enable a very valid use of non-verbal behavior analysis. An interview taking place in a retail store, though, with customers coming and going and workers bustling about would lend itself to great uncertainty when making judgments based on non-verbal behavior. In order to properly utilize non-verbal behavior analysis, it is vital that the interviewer be absolutely sure that the subject is responding only to the stimulus that he is providing.

In Chicago, a couple of years ago, I was in an insurance agency sales office conducting an interview of an insurance agent. A female investigator, Colleen, with whom I work at times, was present during the interview for a specific reason. To negate the distraction of her presence, she seated herself off to the side and slightly back from the subject's normal sight line. She did not speak, write, or make any movements. She simply observed.

As the interview progressed, I noted the subject making a number of grooming gestures. These are unnecessary movements that help to remove stress and anxiety. When people are nervous and anxious, they will generally do one of two things. They will seek to compensate and release pressure by becoming very talkative or by some form of movement. This can include tapping the foot, adjusting glasses, fluffing hair, brushing away imaginary lint from the sleeve, etc. My subject was continually straightening his tie and working on the knot.

I wasn't sure why the subject kept doing that, but the gesture repeated itself many times. I began to study what was causing this particular grooming gesture in comparison to others that he was exhibiting. I wanted to determine what questions and what points were causing that specific motion. After about twenty minutes, I finally identified the stimulus. It was not anything that I was saying or doing. It was not relative to any of the content of the interview. This insurance agent would straighten his tie every time he thought the female investigator in the room was looking at him. He was trying to look nice for Colleen! It had nothing to do with me!

This experience was a perfect illustration of the failings of reliance on non-verbal behavior analysis in all situations. If I had not figured out what was causing this movement, I may have made some very wrong judgments about what was happening in that interview room that day. Indeed, I had begun to believe this was an important gesture. I almost made a serious mistake.

As a footnote here, this was also a good illustration of how the presence of a second person in the interview room can interfere with the process. Despite taking every precaution to lessen that effect, we still encountered a problem.

VERBAL BEHAVIOR ANALYSIS

Verbal behavior analysis is a very different approach. **Verbal Signals** are:

1. More productive and easier to detect than non-verbal.

2. Easier to control by the subject.

This presents the interviewer with a different challenge. Since the subject is better able to control verbal responses, we must increase the sampling that we are working with. This necessitates even more our need to encourage the subject to talk as much as possible. The greater the amount of word production, the less control the subject will have over what those words are.

Verbal behavior analysis offers another important advantage. One must not be physically present to incorporate the technique. We may analyze verbal behavior in written statements, transcripts of recorded interviews, depositions, trial testimony, etc. We may also utilize verbal behavior analysis during telephone interviews. This offers the investigator a great deal more flexibility and benefit than non-verbal analysis.

Lastly, verbal behavior analysis does more than help to detect deception. Verbal behavior offers clues to missing information, relationships between people, emotional dependencies, distancing from sensitive topics, etc. We have a greater wealth of information available to us from this technique and it is far more functional.

Note: It has been shown that 28% of deceptive subjects will make some form of a detectable admission at some point during their initial story. This will occur without the interviewer asking one specific question. It will come about as a linguistic error during the story.

CHAPTER X

The Truth

THE AVERAGE ADULT LIES SEVEN TIMES A DAY!

As we go through life, we are continually confronted with social situations that require some small alteration of the truth which enables us to get through our day. A coworker comes up and says, "How do you like my new tie?" Despite the fact that it's the ugliest thing you've ever seen, you respond, "It looks great! It goes well with the suit." Was that a truthful statement?

You're walking out of the shopping mall after three hours of holiday shopping. Your feet hurt, your back is sore, you're loaded down with huge bags

full of purchases, and your car is parked at the very far end of the lot. As you embark on the long trek with the heavy packages, you encounter an old friend who says, "Hi! How are you?" What do you answer? You say, "Fine! How about yourself?" Was that a truthful statement?

Obviously, it would serve little purpose for you to tell your coworker that you thought his tie was ugly. It would have caused hurt feelings and inserted a wedge in your working and personal relationship for a long time afterward. So, you pay him the desired compliment, make him feel good about himself, and go on with your day.

Your old friend in the parking lot was being polite when he asked you how you were. He didn't really want an answer to that question. Imagine what his reaction would be if you said, "Let me tell you how I'm doing! My feet hurt and my back hurts. I'm so sick of this holiday shopping stuff that I could throw up! No one in my family helps me out with any of this. My in-laws are coming for dinner and I still haven't been to the grocery store. I've got my quarterly reports due at work and my daughter has the flu! Life generally stinks! How about you?"

We all bend the truth in these small ways to help us deal with the social interactions in our lives. These types of lies do not elicit guilt feelings, or bring about anxiety, because they are not intended to be deceptive. They are not meant to conceal any truth of real value. They are only meant to ease us through our day and to eliminate unnecessary explanations of essentially trivial issues.

When it comes to truth, as it relates to topics of importance, most people do not lie. They just won't tell you everything. They manipulate their language in order to be technically truthful, while remaining deceptive.

A suspect in a theft is questioned.

Interviewer: "Did you take the money?"

Subject: "I don't steal!"

Did he deny the theft? Human nature would lead us to give the subject the benefit of the doubt in this situation. We would tend to want to accept this as a denial of his involvement in the theft. But is it? The subject didn't say, "No, I did not take the money!" By using the present tense verb, "don't", he only told the interviewer what he does not do now and perhaps what he will not do in the future. This is not a denial of what he did yesterday, or at any other time in the past. Therefore, we cannot, and must not, accept this as a denial. Using these words, the subject could have stolen the money and remained technically truthful in his response. After all, with this close of a call to getting caught, he may now have no intention of stealing again. His days as a thief are over. Hence the response, "I don't steal!", is a truthful one.

This is why linguistic analysis is so important to the interviewer. People will tell the truth whenever they can. They merely make changes in their language in order to accommodate the truth, while still providing a deceptive response. This reduces anxiety and guilt feelings and, in so doing, also reduces the amount of readable non-verbal behavior we might observe.

The interviewer must approach the interview with an acceptance of belief in what the subject is saying. However, that belief must be limited to the very literal interpretation of the words. "I don't steal!", is NOT a denial when taken in a total literal sense.

A man is questioned about shooting another man in the storage room of an office building.

Interviewer: "Tell me everything that happened."

Subject: "I was standing outside the storage room when I heard a shot. I went to see what happened and I found him dead."

Did this subject deny involvement in the shooting? Did he give any information that would shed light on the possible perpetrator(s)? No, his story was very sketchy at best. The first thing to concern the interviewer here is the fact that there was no denial.

When the physical evidence was accumulated, everything pointed toward the subject as being the assailant. The police were able to prove he fired a gun, had a motive, was in the correct proximity at the time of the shooting, etc. Why then, does the subject make the statement that he does? At first glance it would seem to be a denial. But, is it?

Let's examine what he said. He began with, "I was standing outside the storage room when I heard a shot." If he were the killer and he had fired a gun into the storage room, killing the victim, would this statement have contradicted reality? Certainly if he had fired a gun, he would have, "heard a shot."

Next, he said, "I went to see what happened and I found him dead." If, after shooting the victim and watching him fall, the subject went to be sure that he had successfully killed him, this statement also would not contradict reality. So, for the killer to have made the statement that he did, he actually told the police everything except, "I did it!"

This is not uncommon. Most times a deceptive subject will attempt to mix as much truth as possible into his account. Besides reducing anxiety and guilt, it enables the subject to remember the story better if he has to tell it again at a later date. The subject would need only remember the fictional part and where to insert it, when telling an otherwise truthful account. This would also provide continuity and consistency in his story through time and re-telling.

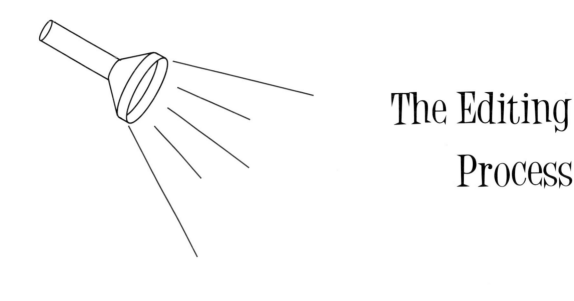

CHAPTER XI

The Editing Process

As an interviewer asks a subject to, "Tell me everything that happened on Saturday," the subject is left with an impossible task. He cannot relate to the interviewer "everything" that happened. That would be far too much information for him to impart. He would have to begin with something like, "Well, I woke up, coughed two times, scratched my head, burped, sat up and blinked six times", etc. Obviously, he cannot do that.

So, what happens? The subject, like all of us, must go through an editing process by which he decides what is important to tell. Since he cannot tell everything, he must make mental judgments about what to include and what to omit. This happens instantly. The subject has no control over what his own personal editing process will produce for him to verbalize when he speaks.

As the mind puts forward the events that the subject will tell, his own personal linguistic code will take over to choose the words which relate this information. This linguistic code is a product of his background, social status, environment, heritage, ethnicity, education, etc. This dictates the words that will express the data that the editing process of his brain has selected to be dispensed.

Everyone has a distinctly personal linguistic code. For instance, if I were to say, "I got up at 6:00 A.M.", what would that mean? Am I out of bed? Was that the time my alarm clock went off? Did I hit the snooze button and relax in bed for another 20 minutes? To some people the term, "got up", means being physically out of bed. To others, it is only the time that they awoke, although they didn't physically get out of bed until some time later. My definition of that is the time that I am physically out of bed. Yet I cannot apply my definition to another person without being sure that they utilize the same meaning for that terminology. If I did, I could be making an important mistake about what that person told me had happened. If a subject said that he "got up at 7:00 A.M.", and by his definition that was only when he awoke, I would need to learn that. If I simply apply my definition, I would have him out of bed and physically active doing something else when he was actually still lying in his bed. This would be an egregious error on my part and an important misinterpretation of the actual facts.

It is this linguistic code that we, as interviewers, have to concentrate on breaking. We need to understand the meanings that the subject has for the words he uses. Our definitions do not apply. Once we have discerned his code, we look for changes in his language and compare them to the events that are being described. Although the subject's mind will involuntarily produce the important events for the subject to relate, this does not ensure that they will be related. The subject is the final arbiter to decide what he will tell. As the mind produces the information to be put into words, the subject must then alter that information if he wants to prevent himself from revealing it. This will also cause an alteration in his language and provide clues for the interviewer to the accuracy of what is being said.

CHAPTER XII

The Memory Centers

The human mind deals with two **Memory Centers.**

1. One center records events.

2. One center determines the language used to verbalize them.

The second one is equipped with a monitoring function that works to assure accuracy. It operates in a very similar fashion to the computer "Spell Checker". As a person remembers an event and begins to relate it, the words go through this "Checker". It will alter language to remain truthful and accurate wherever possible. Only a conscious effort by the subject can prevent this from happening and this is difficult for the subject to do.

This is because the process happens instantly and the subject has little control over it when speaking at a normal conversational pace. Many clues to additional information may be available to the interviewer if he listens carefully to these word choices.

A man is talking about what he did on a Sunday afternoon.

"My two friends came over to watch football. We ordered a pizza, watched the early game and talked over old times. During the second game, we played some cards. They stayed most of the day and then about eight o'clock my friend and his cousin left."

What happened to cause this man to become angry with the cousin? We know that he was. We just don't know why. As the two came over earlier in the day, he described them as "my two friends". When they left, one of them maintained friendship status. The other lost that position and became, "his cousin". This is not an accident or a slip of the tongue. It is a clear change in the subject's own language which gives us additional information about what occurred that Sunday afternoon.

We do have some clues to what that might have been. We know that during the first game, they, "talked over old times". Then as they watched the second game they, "played some cards". Could there have been a problem during the card game that caused the subject to become upset with one of them? That might be possible. It could also be that what transpired is not of any real importance to the interviewer. What is certain, however, is that the interviewer would need to clarify this information to make a determination as to its significance in relationship to the interview purpose.

CHAPTER XIII

Two Basic Questions

As the interviewer works to evaluate the information he is receiving during the interview process, he should have two basic questions in mind. He should consider:

1. Why did the subject say that?

2. Why did the subject say that using those specific words?

Careful analysis of the word choices and the point in the story where they appear is critical. These are the clues that lead to detection of deception and/or missing information.

A woman went to the police to report a rape.

Police Officer: "Tell me everything that happened."

Woman: "I was walking down a dark street and I turned into an alley. A man came out from behind a trash dumpster, put a knife to my throat, and said that if I didn't have sex with him, he would kill me. So, we laid down on the ground and we had sex. Then he ran away."

Does this story sound truthful? What's wrong with what she said here? At first glance, it would seem that there is something not quite right about it, but what is it? Let's look at the story with the above questions in mind.

Beginning with the first few words, we will note that the subject said that she was "walking down a dark street". Note the adjective, "a", that is inserted in the story before the words "dark street". If this is a rape, wouldn't it be one of the most important and terrible events in her life? In that instance, can this really be just "a dark street"? Wouldn't that street have to have an identity? Wouldn't it have to have a name? And, if she didn't know the name, shouldn't it be "the street in front of the theater" or "the street that goes down to the park", or something else to that effect? We must remember that memories contain millions of tiny connections to other things. This street would have to be a very specific street because this was the street that led to the alley where she was raped. She couldn't just call it "a" dark street.

This is continued by her use of the word, "an", in front of the alley that she turned into. That would make it any old alley. Is that possible? Would the victim of a rape describe the alley where it took place as just, "an alley"? No, it would be "the alley behind the barber shop" or "the alley that empties onto Fort Street", or something of that nature. It couldn't be just "an alley"! Real memory connections would not permit the story without adjacent identifiers and details.

Going further into her story, we find another problem. Notice her use of the participatory pronoun, "we". She said, "we laid down", and, "we had sex". Does a rape victim use the word "we"? Is the rape victim a willing participant in the event? No, the rape victim says, "He did that to me!". What is happening is being done "to her", not "with her". The use of the word, "we", denoting her participation, is out of context and should cast doubt on the truth of her statement.

By going over the story and looking at the word choices, we have found that two adjectives, "a" and "an", are inappropriate. Further, we have found the uncharacteristic use of the participatory pronoun, "we", in two critical places. This should lead the interviewer to strongly suspect deception in this story.

There is another point here, and that is that something glaring is missing. The story ends with the rapist running away. There is no mention of what happened afterward. For a rape victim, or any victim of a personal crime, does the story end there? Shouldn't there also be an emotional reaction to what has just happened? In this case, we would have expected that the subject would have continued her story with something like, "I was scared. I got up and dragged myself to a phone and I called my mother. She came and picked me up and took me to the hospital." But she didn't do that.

The absence of this emotional reaction, which is still a large part of the story as far as the subject is concerned, is out of bounds. The fact that it is not there is greater reason for the interviewer to doubt the truthfulness of the story. Coupled with the two misplaced adjectives and the two participatory pronouns, we would have to conclude that the subject is not being truthful here.

This was an actual case. The police, after having analyzed the story, confronted the subject with their doubts. The subject admitted that the story was not true. She had been out with a boyfriend and they had had an argument. He told her to get out of the car and she did. Later, she made up this story to make him feel bad for having dropped her off like he did. She did not expect him to make her go to the police to repeat the story and report it as a crime. When he did, she didn't know what else to do except to continue the lie. By analyzing the words, detecting the deception, and then confronting the subject with it, the police were able to save hundreds of investigative hours searching for a rape suspect that never existed.

The key to this analysis was listening to more than the mere sequence of events. This underscores the necessity of listening to not only the facts, but also the specific words by which the facts are presented.

CHAPTER XIV

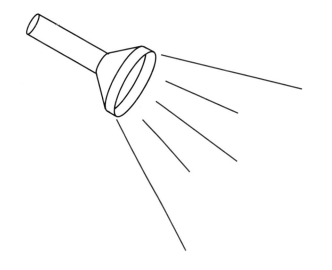

Passive Language – Pronouns

Pronouns are interesting words. They give us responsibility in our language. They are also the words that will produce 90% of the admissions that we will hear, or read, in a story. There are several ways to look at pronoun usage.

1. The Missing "I"

One of the first things to look for is the missing pronoun in a place where you would expect to find one. If the subject were to say to you, "Went shopping", what would that mean? Did he go alone? Did he have someone with him? Who went shopping?

If the subject were to say, "Saw the accident", what does that mean? Did he see the accident? Was he among a group of people who saw the accident? Did someone see the accident and tell him about it? Who saw the accident?

Let's look at a subject's Witness Statement to the police on a specific accident case.

Witness: "Yeah, saw the accident. Saw the accident. The red car came around the corner and hit the blue car."

What is glaringly missing in this statement is the pronoun to tell us who saw the accident. We cannot give the subject the benefit of the doubt and assume that he is referring to himself here. Remember the 3rd Golden Rule! Until a subject says that something happened, it didn't happen! If the subject does not insert the "I" in front of the verb, "saw", we cannot do it for him. We cannot say that he, "saw the accident", until he actually tells us that he did.

In this particular case, the subject did not see the accident. He had been standing on the corner with his girlfriend when the accident happened. He heard the noise, turned to look, and saw the cars in crumpled heaps. His girlfriend was looking in the direction of the accident when it happened and she told him about it. Since he was there, and since he knew exactly what had happened, he became a witness. But is he a credible witness? Should we believe him? Until he inserts the pronoun, "I", in front of his verb, we cannot accept what he says. We must question him further. In this case, when asked to elaborate, the investigator was able to discern that he was not, in fact, a witness.

The subject did not lie, however, in his statement. He never identified WHO had actually seen the accident. He only told us that someone had seen it. Technically, what he said was truthful. If we err and insert the pronoun for him, then that error is ours, not his!

2. The Missing "We"

Similarly, the missing "We" is of great importance. Here we'll examine a subject's description of a shopping trip that he took with his wife.

Subject: "Saturday, the wife and I went to Carlton Mall. I drove and she sat in the passenger seat. I dropped her off at Penney's at one end of the mall and I drove to the other end and parked by Sears. I bought some tools and then met her in the center of the mall. She and I shopped in a couple of small retail stores for an hour or so. I went to Radio Shack and she went to Ganto's. Then she and I walked back to where I had parked the car. I drove home. At the house she got out in front of the garage and I parked in the garage. She had bought some towels and I had purchased some socket wrenches. She went in the house and I stayed in the garage to put my tools away. She sat at the kitchen table and worked on a crossword puzzle and when I came in, I sat there too. She and I sat there for an hour or so and then I went into the living room and so did she. Both of us watched T.V."

This story was odd in that the subject never used the word, "we", during his entire account. Here he goes on a shopping trip with his wife and he elongates his sentences with awkward wording in order to prevent himself from being forced into using the word, "we". What does this mean?

This should cause us to question the relationship between this man and his wife. The word, "we", denotes togetherness and closeness. His inability to use the word should bring us to conclude that there may be some problems in his relationship with his wife. Such problems would preclude his use of any words that evoke a picture of closeness. Thus, the language becomes stilted. The shortest way to give a sentence is the best and most meaningful.

So, do we as interviewers care whether or not this man has a close relationship with his wife? In this case, she was dead and he was the suspect in her murder. Did this information just become more important?

3. Pronouns That Come Before Identifying Who the Person Is

What do we do when we are in a room with other people and someone new enters the room? We introduce the new person to the rest of the group. That is correct social behavior.

A statement, or a story, is no different. When we are telling about something that happened and we introduce a new person into the story, correct social behavior would be to identify that person for our listeners. It would not be too dissimilar from saying something like, "Meet John Doe, Mary's husband."

So what does it mean when a subject uses a pronoun to bring a person into a story before identifying who that person is?

Subject: "I was sitting at the kitchen table having coffee with Bob when she came into the room. She went to the stove and poured herself some tea. Then she got some toast and pulled up a chair at the table with Bob and I. She just didn't want us to be able to talk in private."

This story definitely omits the proper social introduction that we would expect from the subject. Why does he tell us what "she" did and not tell us who "she" is? When this happens, we must consider that there may be a strain in the relationship between the subject and the person about whom he is speaking. Why is he having difficulty using her name? Why does he not properly introduce her? It is very likely that there is stress between these two people and it may have an impact on the matter at hand. The interviewer needs to recognize this and question the subject further regarding the relationship.

4. Plural Pronouns

Plural pronouns can work to deceive the interviewer when they occur where they would not be expected.

Subject: "Mark and I went to a party at a house on Maxwell Street. We only stayed there for a couple of hours and I only had a couple of beers. Then we drove over to the Last Call Grill, where we stayed until closing. Then we drove home."

I don't know what kind of car the subject and Mark were driving, but it must have been quite unique in its operating controls. My car, for example, only has one steering wheel and, "we", can't drive! I can drive, or you can drive. But "we" cannot!

What would cause the subject to make this alteration with a plural pronoun? We do know that he stated that he, "only had a couple of beers." However, his inclusion of this information, if it were not in response to a question involving alcohol intake, would indicate that he was concerned with the amount of beer he had consumed. He next addresses leaving the party and going to a bar. The question of who was driving comes into play and he suddenly gives us a plural pronoun, which we know is impossible, but it does work to block this information from the story. He could have said that he and Mark, "went to the Last Call Grill." That would have eliminated any discussion over who was driving and, therefore, any concerns over intoxication as it relates to operating a motor vehicle. He didn't choose to do that, though. He went straight to the issue and then made an instant adjustment which prevented us from knowing who actually operated the car.

This type of manipulation through the utilization of a plural pronoun should bring the interviewer to question further the information that was just imparted. The interviewer would need to recognize this and question the subject to obtain clarification. What absolutely must not happen, however, is the interviewer ignoring what he just heard and giving the subject the benefit of the doubt. We must only believe exactly what we hear.

5. Too Many "I"s

This is an anomaly that always fascinates me. This is the subject who takes full credit for virtually everything. When this subject speaks, the "I" is omnipresent everywhere.

Subject: "I woke up and I got dressed. I went to the kitchen and I made myself some breakfast. I ate my breakfast. I cleaned up the dishes and I went out to the garage. I opened the garage door and I got into my car. I backed out of the driveway and I drove to work because I always want to be at work on time. At work, things went okay and everything was finished promptly. Coworkers assisted quite a bit on some of the projects and a lot of work was completed. Then I drove home and I parked the car in the garage. I went into the house and I made myself some dinner before I watched T.V."

Why does this subject use the "I" to such an extreme? The first thing that the interviewer needs to understand is that this is a part of the subject's linguistic code. This is the way in which the subject speaks normally. Therefore, we will have to accept this as an operational fact and look for the variances that may, or may not, occur. The window into this subject's personality is unusual. When the subject deviates from the "I", the interviewer will know that that point in the story is sensitive and that that information is important.

What happened with our subject in this example? Upon his arrival at work, his verbiage became passive as things were accomplished with little or no identification of who was accomplishing them. The "I" disappeared while he was at work, but it returned in full force when he left work. This should cause the interviewer to examine which may have transpired at

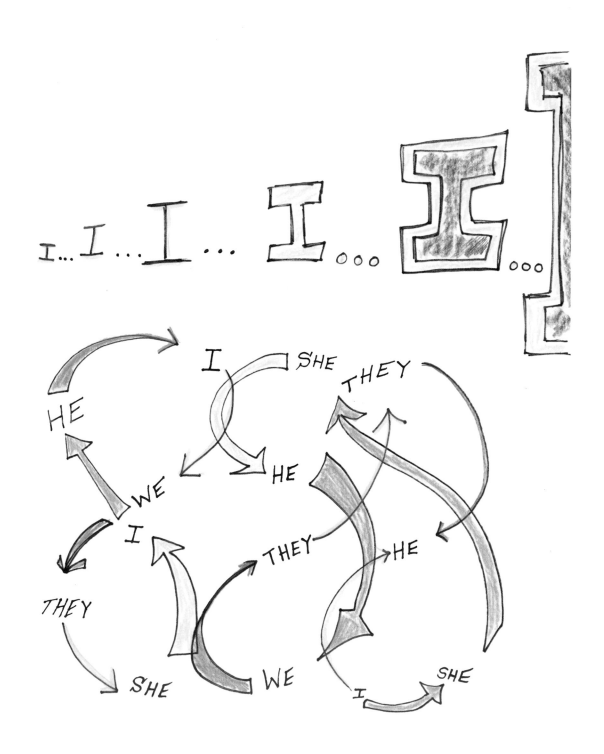

work that caused the subject to abandon his normal linguistic code and leave the "I" behind.

6. Possessive Pronouns

Possessive pronouns give us ownership and control. They personalize things for us and bring us closer to the persons or things that they accompany. Let's look at a subject's statement about a stolen car.

Subject: "I was driving this red Corvette north on I-75 around 12 Mile Road when I passed a hitchhiker. He was a real raunchy looking guy and he stared at the car as I sped by. I continued north on I-75 to the 14 Mile Road Exit, where I got off the expressway and turned into the Oakland Mall parking lot. I looked for a safe place to park the car and I ended up parking next to a large sign with the letter, "G", on top. I thought that would be a great place since I always seem to forget where I park. I went into the mall and shopped for a couple of hours. When I came out, the car was gone. I was sure that I went and looked at the correct spot under the big, "G". But the car was gone. Somebody stole the car!"

What's missing from this story? The question here is whether or not this is the subject's company car, a rental car, or a borrowed car. What we do know for certain is that it is not HIS car. How do we know this? Not once did the subject use the possessive pronoun, "my". Owning a really fine car is a personal gratification. If we own a Corvette, is it just, "the car"? No! It is, "my car"! If our car is stolen, do we say, "Somebody stole THE car!" No! That would be, "Somebody stole MY car!" This is a personal thing and possessive pronouns are used to personalize those connections as we take ownership. Therefore, in understanding this, the interviewer already knows one more piece of information than the subject thinks he does. Further, it should lead the interviewer to question why the subject chose to cloud the issue of ownership.

7. Pronoun Changes

Think of any time in your past, any event that occurred. Think about what you were doing, where you were, and who was there. As you do this, are you alone or is someone else there? Are you confused about this? Are we ever confused about whether we are alone or with someone else?

So why does a person say...?

Subject: "We,...ah,...I went to the mall."

   OR

Subject: "I,...ah,...we met with the client."

Is this possible? Can the subject be confused about whether or not he is alone? What happened here? What does this mean?

This should bring us to consider another important principle.

A change in the subject's language... = ...a change in the subject's reality!

Since the subject cannot be confused about whether he is alone or with someone, then we must conclude that this change in his language represents an alteration of the truth that he is imparting in his story. And since there is no reason to stumble over these words, we must also conclude that the change is conscious and intentional on the part of the subject.

CHAPTER XV

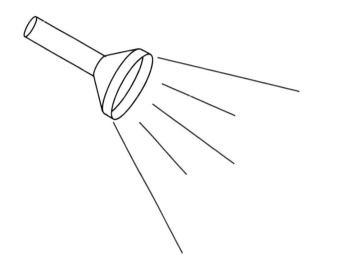

Passive Language – Verbs

Verbs are the frame of information in a story. Alteration of verb tense permits the subject to bypass the formula of first person, singular, past tense that is necessitated by relating a story of something that has happened. In doing this, a subject may give us information that is technically truthful and yet continues to deceive.

A subject is being questioned about a theft from the Controller's Office of his plant. Some money has been stolen from a cash box in a desk drawer. He responds:

Subject: "I don't go into the office part of the building. That's for supervisory personnel only. And, besides, I would never steal any money!"

Using these words, the subject appears to be denying any involvement in the crime. But is he? Did he actually say that he didn't do it? Let's examine his words.

First, the subject offers us an objection. He says, "I don't go into the office part of the building." Is that the same thing as, "I did not go into the office part of the building."? The verb tense is different. It is not in the past tense and therefore cannot be accepted. It does not say what the subject did in the past. It only states his position on the matter as of right now. We would term this as an, "objection", because it only seeks to argue whether or not you should believe he did it based on a peripheral fact. He "objects"! Instead of attacking the issue of the theft, he seeks to dismiss himself as a suspect by arguing lack of opportunity. But, even so, he does not do so convincingly because he does not use the past tense verb, "didn't".

The second sentence continues the argument against opportunity by restating the company policy on entrance into the office area of the plant. He seeks to convince us that he couldn't have had the opportunity to steal the money because company policy prohibits him from entering the office area. This is, of course, rather ludicrous when we look at it closely. The subject is, in effect, saying that he couldn't be the thief because he couldn't break company policy to enter the necessary area. We are to believe that he is more adherent to the company policy regarding his access to certain parts of the plant, than he is to company policy against theft! Since we know that a person speaks about what is most important to him first, we would have to conclude by this that the subject perceives trespassing into the restricted area as a greater wrong than stealing. Logically, that would not make much sense. So, we have to consider why else he would speak of access to the office area before he speaks to the issue of the theft. This can only be a furthering of the objection.

The last sentence is crucial. The subject begins it by saying, "And, besides,...". That is to say that the theft issue is almost an afterthought to the subject. Then, he continues by saying, "...I would never steal any money!" Notice the verb tense here. It is in future tense. The subject is not telling us what he did or did not do in the past. He is not even speaking to his actions in the present. He is telling us that in the future he would not steal, and that is very different from a denial of an action in the past.

Consequently, we cannot accept this subject's statement as any form of denial of his involvement in the theft. That should bring us to question him more closely on this issue. We would normally expect an innocent person to deny his involvement first, before doing, or saying, another thing. At the very least, we would expect a denial to appear at some point. The complete absence of ANY denial should bring us to conclude that something is very wrong here.

Examination of verb tense in this way can give the interviewer valuable additional insight into what the subject is really saying. Acknowledging that the subject will attempt to be truthful, we can expect to find verbiage alterations as a means to permit technical truth for the subject while creating deception for the listener.

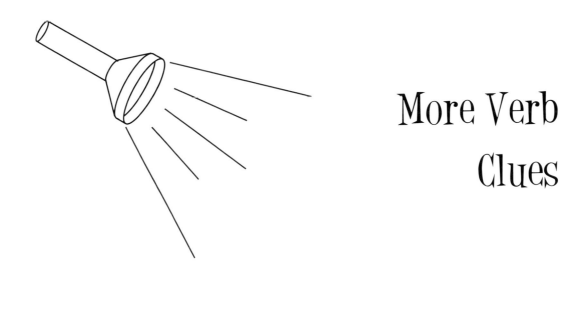

CHAPTER XVI

More Verb Clues

There are additional clues that may be gleaned from the way a subject uses his verbs. We will examine some of the more common clues that may occur as a person tells us a story.

1. Think/Believe

These words come to us as an "Escape Clause". They are words which precede a portion of information that the subject is not committed to. When a subject says, "*I think* the car was red...," he is avoiding offering a commitment to the accuracy of this information. Sometimes this is done in an honest effort by the subject so as not to mislead the interviewer with facts that he is not sure of. Other times, however, it is a cue that the subject just wants to put some distance between himself and the declaration that he has just made. If it was a lie, this would reduce anxiety and stress for the subject. Additionally, it would allow him an "out" if he is ever confronted with the real truth. He can then say that he never told the interviewer that he was sure of this information. He only "thought" it was true.

The word, "believe", is much the same. A subject stating, "I believe that it was ten o'clock...," is also dodging commitment. Therefore, the interviewer must not significantly rely upon the accuracy of any information that follows either of these words.

2. Started/Finished – Began/Ended

When one of these words appears in a story, the interviewer must look for the other word to pair it up with. If a task is accomplished, we have no reason to say any more than something like, "I did the dishes!". Why would the subject need to say more? If the subject were to tell us only half of this equation, however, it offers us a great deal more information. Let's look at an example.

Interviewer: "What happened when you got home from work?"

Subject: "Well, I came in the house, grabbed a beer out of the refrigerator, and then went into the laundry room and finished the laundry. Then I made some dinner and watched T.V. until about eleven o'clock. Then I went to bed."

Notice the use of the word, "finished", here. It is not complete because it does not have its partner, "started", in the story. Why does the subject tell us that he "finished" the laundry without telling us about "started"? We automatically know that one of two things is true here. First, someone else may have "started" the laundry because the subject only "finished" it. Alternatively, the subject may actually have "started" the laundry at a previous time and only "finished" it at this time.

If neither of these things were true, the subject would have said that he, "...went into the laundry room and did the laundry." But he did not say that. He only said that he "finished" the laundry. By noticing this word usage, we find additional information that needs clarification.

Why would the interviewer care about when, or by whom, the laundry was "started"? Maybe he wouldn't. But the one thing we know for sure is that it IS important for the subject to make a differentiation between the two, and therefore, the interviewer must take the responsibility to find out why.

In this case, maybe the laundry was "started" by another person, such as his wife. He came home from work and he found the laundry not "finished". This necessitated that he complete the task and perhaps that was not to his liking. So, he said that he "finished" the laundry rather than "did" the laundry because his anger at his wife for not completing the job earlier forced him to point out that he had to "finish" it for her.

Whatever the reason, it is incumbent on the interviewer to sort it out and find the reason behind the subject's word choices. If one of these words appears without its partner, we must examine why this occurred.

3. Remember

When a person tells us a story, what is it that he is telling us? He is telling us about something that has already happened. In order to do that, he must access memory for the information. What the person says is, in effect, what he remembers!

With that in mind, what brings a person to say "I remember" during the story? If what the person is relating is something that has happened in the past, then the person is already telling us what he "remembers". In order to tell it, he must "remember" it! So, when a person uses the words, "I remember", within a story, he is actually saying, "I remember that I remember!" That is illogical!

Subject: "I went to the Sheep Tavern Restaurant for some dinner. When I arrived there, I pulled into the west parking lot and parked next to a Ford Bronco, and I remember it was white."

This subject is talking about an event in the past. It is what he remembers. So, why does he use the word, "remember", within the story? It would be enough for him to tell us that the Ford Bronco was white. We would assume that that information came from memory. But the subject chose to add an extra emphasis on the color being white, as if to say, "I'm really sure that it was white!". Why?

This happens because the subject is trying to assure that the interviewer understands that this information is very important for him to impart and he wants to be sure that the interviewer got it. It is the subject's way of adding tremendous emphasis to this information. He is highlighting it, putting asterisks, quotation marks, parentheses, etc. on it. He wants to be certain that it is heard and noted. This information is very important for the subject to relay to the interviewer.

Is it also then important for the interviewer to know? It may be. It may not be. It may mean nothing to the interviewer then or later. But we do know that, for the subject, it IS important and that fact makes it noteworthy to follow up on. The question becomes, "Why was it important for the subject to say that?"

CHAPTER XVII

Why?

When a person relates a story, he tells us what happened. We expect him to tell us what he did, but not why he did it. When the "why?" question is answered for us, without or before a question, then the interviewer must pay attention to that piece of information.

Interviewer: "Tell me about your injury."

Subject: "I was working on the forklift at work and I fell as I climbed down. I hurt my lower back. I reported it to the foreman and I was sent home. The next day I went to see a doctor. I chose Dr. Smith because he has a fine reputation. He wrote me a slip for disability and I haven't worked since."

In this case, the interviewer did not ask the subject why he went to Dr. Smith. He only asked what happened. The subject, in his narrative, chose to include the extra information about why he selected Dr. Smith to go to. This is out of bounds of the question. "Why" he went there is not what was asked. The interviewer must conclude that this information is sensitive and important information.

Perhaps what the subject would have said, had he continued, is, "I chose Dr. Smith because he has a fine reputation. He vouches for disability for 29 of my friends, so I knew he'd do it for me." Whatever the rest of the story is, the interviewer must note the importance of the addition of the, "why", into the story when it was not asked.

Take another example:

Subject: "I paid with cash because I'm old fashioned."

If the subject's reasoning was not asked, then why was it added? Did the subject anticipate a request for a receipt that he did not have, or does not exist? Whenever an interviewer is confronted with an answer to a "why" question that was never asked, it must be treated as sensitive and important information.

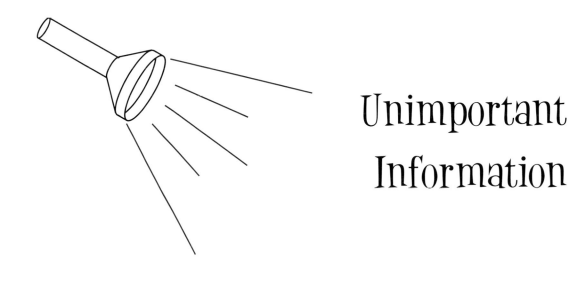

CHAPTER XVIII

Unimportant Information

As we discussed, understanding the function of the Editing Process is vital in analyzing information that we receive. It is this procedure that brings a person to make choices about what is important to be included in the story. Taking that into consideration, the interviewer is able to learn much more than what the subject may have intended. In the following example, we will take an excerpt of a response by a subject in answer to the interviewer's question.

Interviewer: "Tell me everything that happened from the time you got up until the time you went to sleep on Saturday."

Subject: "...I got in my car and went to my Aunt Martha's house. On the way there, I stopped at the Florist to buy her some flowers. I decided to get carnations and I bought her pink, because she really likes pink!..."

In this example we have a subject describing a trip to Aunt Martha's house as a part of his story about what happened on that Saturday. In telling us about it, he included a stop along the way during which he bought her some flowers. He goes on to tell us what kind of flowers he purchased and even tells us what color he chose. Assuming that the reason for this inquiry has nothing to do with the purchase of the flowers, the interviewer has to ask himself a question. Why did the subject report the color and the reason for the color choice in his statement? Is it likely that Aunt Martha's fondness for pink is an important piece of information to the story? Probably not! So, why is it noted?

This takes us back to the concept of the Editing Process. The subject is reporting to us everything that happened as dictated by the editing portion of his memory. When things happen to us in real life, they are recorded in there and have countless strands of connections to other things. These memory connections are hard to separate. Thus, this subject cannot tell us about purchasing flowers for his Aunt Martha without also telling us what color he bought and why. These things are all linked in his memory and are not reportable independently.

What does this mean to the interviewer? It is a good indication that the information being given there is truthful. Nothing happens in a vacuum. A story that is fabricated comes to us heavily laden with facts and devoid of any unimportant connections to other things and/or events. Therefore, when we find these pieces of unimportant information within a story, we must deem their very existence as important. Their inclusion goes to evidence of truthfulness at the points in the story where they appear.

Interviewer: "What kind of bicycle was it?"

Subject: "It was a Schwinn. It reminded me a lot of one that I had when I was a kid. The handlebars had the same kind of curve to them where they joined the fork, and I remember that it made it difficult to mount my AM/FM radio bracket where I had wanted to put it."

In this example we see that the subject did not just answer the question, but went on to draw a comparison to another bicycle that he remembered from his past. This need to bring in his memory connection to a piece of information that was not likely important for the interviewer to know lends itself greatly to the truthfulness of what the subject said.

Unimportant information relates to memory connections. Its existence inside a story is a visible clue that must be noted.

CHAPTER XIX

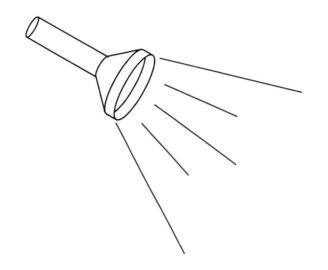

Rate of Speech and Looping

The rate of speech at which a subject speaks should be a gauge that is monitored carefully by the interviewer. As in all evaluations of a person's language as he communicates, the interviewer must first establish the subject's "norm". Next, the interviewer should observe the pattern during the course of the interview to determine if any changes occur. Does the subject slow down? Does he speed up? Are his words clumped together? Are there large gaps between phrases? All of these things are important observations and may key the interviewer in on the subject's editing of information and/or deception.

Slower rate of speech will generally occur when the subject is trying to be careful. He is attempting to weigh each word to avoid making a mistake.

This may happen when the subject gets to a point in his story which is sensitive or where he wishes to move past a part that he doesn't want to tell. It may also happen if the subject is trying to lie to the interviewer. Whatever the reason behind it, the subject is definitely making every effort to control the information that he is imparting.

A faster rate of speech is usually caused by nervousness. The subject has just come to a point which is highly sensitive to him. He speeds up in an effort to move past it. This should serve as a cue to the interviewer to bring the subject back to this point later in the interview and take him through it very slowly.

It is expected that the subject's rate of speech may change with emotional changes that occur as the interview moves from one topic to another. Possibly, the interviewer may touch on a sensitive issue for the subject that evokes an emotional response. That would, of course, be likely to affect the subject's rate of speech. Understanding that, the interviewer may ignore occurrences that can be explained. He must remain continually watchful, however, for any changes that occur without explanation. If we understand why the subject's rate of speech has been altered, then it probably is not important to us. What we need to be wary of are those times which we cannot explain. It is there that the interviewer may find a clue to important and sensitive information.

Sometimes a variance in the rate of speech will be accompanied by another strange aberration. Unexplainably, the interviewer may notice that the subject continuously covers one point, over and over. Upon completion of that portion of his story, he goes back to the beginning and tells it again whenever an interview question allows him to reconnect to it. In effect, he is "looping" back to one specific scene and replaying it for the interviewer. Why does a subject do that?

Essentially, the subject believes that that portion of his story is significant, and he truly wants the interviewer to remember it. It may be true. It may not be true. Looping, in and of itself, offers no guarantee of the presence or absence of deception. What it does do, however, is offer the interviewer a window into the subject's mind and what is important to him. This should bring the interviewer to more closely examine that part of the story.

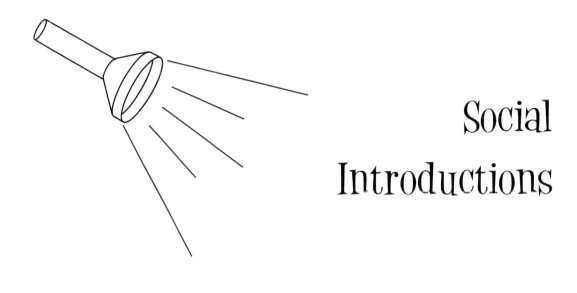

CHAPTER XX

Social Introductions

When a person enters a room, it is only polite to introduce him to the other people there. A statement is not so different from such a real life experience. When a subject is telling us a story about something that has happened to him, he introduces us to the characters in the story. They will usually enter the story chronologically. They may enter the story alone or in groups of two or more. It is the manner in which they enter the story, however, that is critically important to the interviewer.

When a new person comes into a story, the subject should complete an introduction to the listener/reader. This person should be identified in some manner. For example, if a man is talking about being in his kitchen when his wife enters the room, he should introduce us to his wife. There are several ways by which he could do this. He could say:

A. "My wife came into the room."
B. "My wife, Mary, came into the room."
C. "The wife came into the room."
D. "Mary came into the room."
E. "She came into the room."

In, A., the subject has identified the woman who came into the room as his wife. In, B., he goes further and tells us his wife's name. These would both be acceptable and expected social introductions to the new character entering the story.

In, C., the subject also properly introduces us to the person entering the room, but gives an additional clue to the relationship by his exchange of the word, "my", for the adjective, "the". By calling her "the wife" instead of "my wife", the subject has actually denied her of her position. Though the lack of the possessive pronoun, "my", is very important, the subject will be deemed to have made a correct social introduction for purposes of this chapter.

In, D., the subject is also specific in introducing us to the new person in the story. He just didn't go far enough to define the relationship.

In, E., the subject introduces his wife by the use of the pronoun, "she". This is very important as this is an improper social introduction. It could be indicative of stress in the relationship between he and his wife. It would be very important that the interviewer, when formulating questions, does not assume the identity of, "she". The interviewer must call this new person in the story, "she", just as the subject has until the subject identifies who she is. For the interviewer, it is very valuable to listen to see how long the subject continues to call her by pronoun before he finally identifies her correctly. Then, the point in the story that causes

him to make the change and give her her identity should be noted, as it could be an important point. The change in language must have been precipitated by something; the interviewer must discern what brought that something about.

As we listen to a subject introduce new people to the story, another thing to be considered is the order of their appearance. In very general terms it can be said that the order in which people are introduced into a story reflects the order of their importance in the subject's own life. If a subject tells us that three friends came over and then names them as, "Tom, Ben, and David," we can make an educated guess about the subject's relationship with them. It is very likely that the subject likes, "Tom", best, "Ben", second, and "David", third and/or that this is the order of their priority in the subject's own life.

CHAPTER XXI

Unnecessary Connections

When a subject is telling a story, how does he connect each individual event that occurs? Does he end one event with the completion of the describing sentence before beginning a new sentence for the next event? Does he simply flow from event to event in an uneven, haphazard fashion? Is there a pause between occurrences? Does he utilize words such as **"After"** and **"Left"**?

In the following story, the subject was asked to relate everything that happened on a specific Saturday, from the time he got up until the time he had lunch.

Subject: "I got up, took a shower, and got dressed. I went downstairs into the kitchen and had a glass of orange juice. Then I left the kitchen and went into the living room and sat down to read the newspaper."

When asked to relate, "everything that happened", the subject must enter into the editing process in order to select those events that he feels are important. As his mind chooses which events to include in the story, he has precious little time to make conscious choices about whether to speak the information that his mind has brought forward from memory. If he does not wish to reveal certain recalled important information, he must remove it from the flow which his mind has produced to be related. This is a conscious effort to remove details and/or deceive.

In the above example, the subject utilized an odd connection between two events. After he finished telling us about having "a glass of orange juice", he then told us that he went "into the living room and sat down to read the paper". What is notable here is that he told us that he "left the kitchen". If he went into the living room, we have to know that he left the kitchen. So, why does the subject say this in this way? This would not be important if the subject used this kind of wording for all of his activities. If he had said that he "left the bedroom" before telling us about coming downstairs, it would be of less value to note it the second time. This could be a pattern of his regular speech. The fact that this usage is a CHANGE in his language is what makes it important.

Why did this happen? As the subject was relating the important events as produced through the editing process of his memory, he must have come upon an event or piece of information that he consciously did not want to reveal. He removed it from his story and, in so doing, created a void or empty area that needed to be filled. He thus inserted "left the kitchen". The use of the word, "left", in this way is a good indication of missing information.

While the interviewer must make a mental note of the fact that this occurred at this precise point in the story, he must NOT interrupt the subject for clarification. The subject must be permitted to continue his story unimpeded. When the story is completed and the interviewer begins detailing the inquiry, he must take the subject back to the event that

included the use of the word, "left", and proceed to elicit greater detail to that part of the story.

In this example, the interviewer took the subject back to the part of the story where he was drinking the orange juice. The interviewer started the subject off by saying: "Okay, you're in the kitchen, drinking the orange juice. What happened next?" The subject attempted to continue the story with his movement into the living room, but the interviewer did not allow that. The interviewer continuously brought the subject back for minute detail after minute detail of every event in the kitchen until the subject finally admitted that he had received a phone call. He had not wanted to give this information initially and was forced into revealing it by the patience and detailing of the interviewer.

That phone call was an extremely important piece of information for the interviewer and, having had no knowledge that it existed, he would never have known to ask a question about it. By having the subject tell his story before any questions were asked, and understanding the implication of the subject's usage of the word, "left", in this way, the interviewer was able to uncover a critical piece of information.

The word, "after" can work in the same way. A subject talking about what happened on a given afternoon said:

Subject: "I was standing in the parking lot at the hamburger joint talking to a couple of guys and, after that, I went to Mark's house."

The use of the word, "after", in this way is another indication of missing information. Other indicators might be: **"Next"**, **"Sometime Later"**, **"Shortly Thereafter"**, etc. Connections of these kinds must not be ignored. When they are noted, the interviewer must follow up with very detailed questioning on the parts of the story where they are found. They are very strong indications of possible missing information and/or deception.

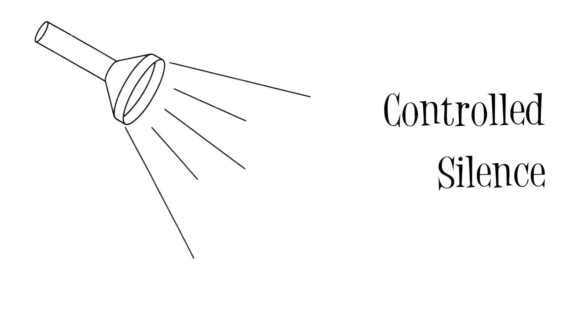

CHAPTER XXII

Controlled Silence

We begin our interviews by asking the subject to relate the pure version of the story. We employ every technique possible to prompt the subject to talk without limitations. We avoid asking any specific questions as we wish the subject to choose for himself that which is important to tell. The subject does, after all, have a story to tell, and that is a fact that the interviewer must keep in mind.

As we go through life, we interview countless people on all sorts of subjects. In our professional lives, we will interview thousands of people in the course of our work. Yet there is a very large difference between being the interviewer and the interviewee, and the interviewer very often does not consider that.

As the professional interviewer, we have a focus on the extraction of information from the subject. We have a veritable clinical approach to this as we have little or no personal interest or involvement in the process. The subject, however, who is imparting the information for us to collect may have a vested interest in controlling that which he imparts. This prompts the subject to mentally prepare for the interview due to its personal effect upon him. As such, the subject not only has a story to tell, but he also knows in advance what part of the story, and how much of it, he intends to reveal. He will have rehearsed it in his mind from the very moment that he is aware of his participation in this interview process to the moment of the interview itself. This rehearsal can take place in minutes, or even seconds. If given advance notice of the interview, the subject could have days or weeks to prepare. Whatever the time allotted, the subject WILL be prepared with a story to tell.

Consider an employee who oversleeps one morning and arrives late at his office. He goes to his desk and begins to work. As he looks up and sees his supervisor approaching, anxiety rises within him and he knows that he will have to explain his tardiness. In an instant, he prepares his response to the inevitable question, "Why were you late this morning?" Upon thinking to himself, he realizes that oversleeping is not going to be an acceptable excuse. This prompts some creativity as he looks at the "drop down menu" of excuse choices in his brain and makes a selection.

When the supervisor arrives at his desk, the inevitable question is asked. The employee begins to describe the traffic accident that he saw on his way to work which had so greatly impaired traffic flow and caused him to be late. He adds details involving the makes and models and colors of the cars, etc., in order to make the story more believable. He tells the story without hesitation and does so quite well. It is hard to believe that he is able to concoct the story so quickly.

The truth is, though, that he was already somewhat prepared with choices as soon as he knew that he was going to be late. He had already selected several options but had not yet decided upon which option to use as he was hoping that his tardiness would go unnoticed. When he was caught, however, he merely had to select one of his many choices and embellish upon it. Details, he reasons, will make the story ring true to the supervisor. There are lots of details which are created instantaneously as he tells his story. When he is done, he sits back, satisfied that he has dealt with his situation very well and awaits the supervisor's responsive questions.

It is at this point in this interview, or any interview, that the interviewer should employ **Controlled Silence.** The subject has finished his prepared story and has nothing else to say. He expects questions and is preparing to answer them by anticipating what they might be and selecting choices to utilize in his responses. What he is NOT expecting is silence.

The interviewer is under no obligation to begin speaking now that the story is finished. As human beings, we are very uncomfortable with si-

lence. Once the subject ends his story, we feel that we should talk. The interviewer does NOT have to talk, though, and should not give in to this urge. The only thing that he must do is let the subject know that he is paying attention and listening. He can do this by maintaining eye contact and tilting his head, shifting in his chair or altering his standing position, leaning back, etc.

This brings both participants into the great void of silence. The subject is waiting for a response to his story from the interviewer and the interviewer is waiting for the subject to continue with his story. The interviewer has the advantage here. He knows what is happening and why. The subject only knows that he has finished his prepared story and does not understand why the interviewer is not speaking. The silence may seem to last a lifetime, but as interviewers, we can wait it out because we know that eventually, the subject WILL speak again. It is inevitable. The pressure of the silence will engulf him and he will feel a need to fill it with words. The only way to do that is to elaborate upon his story by expanding on what happened and providing more details. It is at this point in the interview that the subject will provide some of the most important information and clues to deception and/or missing information. He is now speaking without preparation and this type of improvisation is very difficult for him to edit. It is here that the supervisor will most likely determine the falsity of the employee's traffic accident story.

Controlled Silence can be a critical tool in our search to uncover additional information and clues in an interview. It is a very strong weapon in our interviewing arsenal.

PART 3

Detailing the Inquiry

CHAPTER XXIII

Specific Questions

When we begin an interview, we have issues and questions that beg answering. As previously discussed, we may have lists of questions written down; or we may simply have listed them in our minds. Whichever the method, we do have questions.

Conducting an interview in the manner discussed here has caused us to shelve our questions in the interest of allowing the subject to choose that which is most important for him to reveal. We want the subject to impart information freely, without any guidance from the interviewer as to what he should say. Upon the completion of this process, we will find that the subject will have already answered most of our questions and will have even added additional information that we may not have known to ask about. As we go about detailing the inquiry, one thing is for certain and must be remembered.

Information that is obtained by the interviewer as an answer to a specific question is less reliable than information that comes without a question.

With that in mind, the interviewer should proceed to detail the account that he has just heard. It is at this time that the interviewer may ask questions from his list. It is here that he will clarify any confusion about what the subject may have said. Undoubtedly, many, many questions will have arisen as a result of listening to the subject's story. It is now that the interviewer will work to clarify and define the information thus far received, as well as to obtain answers to the original questions with which he began the interview. Even so, there are pitfalls in how the questions are asked. Certain guidelines must be maintained.

1. Be careful of known facts!

During the course of listening to the subject's story, we begin to form opinions about the truth of what we are hearing. Further, we begin to get a sense of what the subject has said occurred. As the interviewer attempts to detail the information, it is crucial that he does not make a mistake regarding known facts. He must be extremely careful not to make any assumptions regarding what he has heard and not to ask a question that is not based on a true fact.

Consider this case of a woman who was being questioned about the death of her husband. He had just been released from jail a few days before and had been found shot, stabbed, and blown up in his car. The woman and her mother were suspected of conspiring to murder him for the large insurance policy of which she was the named beneficiary. In her story, she mentioned that her husband's brother had been involved in an illegal drug deal and had stolen both the drugs and the money, much to the consternation of the two men with whom he had been partners. Later in her story, while talking about ever present suspicions in the neighborhood that she was involved in her husband's murder, she mentioned having received, "threats", at her home. The interviewer confused the two stories and asked a question.

Interviewer: "What kind of threats?"

Subject: "People coming to my door."

Interviewer: "Describe the two men who came to your door."

What just happened here? At what point did the subject ever say that two men came to her door? The interviewer had mixed up the facts concerning two completely different incidents. He had coupled the drug deal rip-off with neighborhood threats. The result was a question that was totally devoid of any foundation in fact. What was even more interesting in this case was the subject's response. She went on to describe the two men! Why?

The subject in this instance had lost track of her own story. When the interviewer made the erroneous connection between the drug dealers and the neighbors, the subject was mixed up also. She was not sure what she had already said. So, when confronted with this new question, she answered it. She gave very detailed descriptions of the "two men" who came to her door. This became a given event and, forever afterward, she would tell the story of the two men who came to her door and threatened her. The only trouble is, the incident never happened. It was created in response to a mistaken assumption by the interviewer combined with the subject's own doubts about what she had previously said.

Let's examine what she DID say. She said, "People coming to my door." What does that really mean? The first word, "people", is a non-gender specific noun. It is neither male nor female. So, in reality, we do not know if it was men or women or both who came to her door. If the subject was clear on the matter, wouldn't she have said "men" or "women" or "a man and a woman" or something of that nature? Why would she utilize this noun which prevents us from knowing what the gender of the "people" is?

The next important word to examine here is the verb, "coming". What exactly does that mean? It does not describe a single event, as the word implies a constant flow of "people". It depicts an ongoing action and could produce an image of a line of "people" taking turns "coming" to her door and threatening her. This would create an image of numerous "people" in a continual process of threatening the subject at her door. What it does not do, however, is state that "two men" came to her door in a single event and threatened her.

In this case, the interviewer made a critical mistake with his questioning. He caused the creation of a fictional incident and lost an opportunity to obtain additional information and detect possible deception.

2. Listen to and analyze the responses before asking the next question.

Already deeply into the interview at this point, the interviewer is often packed full of questions that he now wants to ask. This leads to a natural tendency to rush from question to question without carefully considering what the response is and/or what it means. This can be a very devastating mistake in the interview process. We must never relax our listening ear or our analytical minds in favor of eliciting fact after fact. Too much information will be lost in the process.

In the same case of the woman and her mother being suspected of conspiring to murder the woman's husband, the interviewer asked another important question.

Interviewer: "Have you heard any talk around town that people think that you or your mother were involved in the death of John Smith?"

Subject: "No. Not before he died!"

Interviewer: "Is there any reason that you can think of for people to think that you or your mother were involved?"

What just happened here? Did the interviewer miss something? The second question is a fine question, but was it appropriate at this point? Didn't the subject just make a mistake that needed to be capitalized upon?

The subject gave, after all, an incredible response to the initial question. At first reading, we may even find it quite humorous. Let's examine what the subject has actually told us. First, she replied with a denial. Then, she coupled that with a time period for that denial during which she had not "heard any talk around town". By saying that "before he died" she had not "heard any talk around town", she has given us two very important pieces of information. She has presented us with two distinct time periods during which this could have happened, and she has told us during which one that it did not happen. Therefore, we have to know that she did, in fact, hear the "talk around town" after "he died".

The curious question here is how she could conceive of a time "before he died" when she could have "heard any talk around town". Certainly if he was not yet dead, no one would be talking about her and/or her mother as being involved in his murder. How could they? He wasn't dead. It was a non-event. Nothing had happened to talk about. Yet, the subject sees this in two distinct parts, the **before** and the **after,** and that could only occur if both were possible.

We can understand how the subject would consider the **after** as a possibility. What we must ask is how the **before** could exist in her mind. The only possible explanation would be if the subject were to include the planning stages of the murder as a part of the whole. Then the subject would have to consider that she and/or her mother may have been talked about **before** the murder by someone who may have suspected, or had actual knowledge, of what they were planning to do. After all, if she were not involved in the planning, there could be no **before** for her. Considering this, she decided that she had not heard anything connecting her and/or her mother to the conspiracy planning **before** he was killed. She only heard the talk **after** the actual murder. That the subject could see the possibility of talk **before** the event is tantamount to an admission of involvement in the murder.

The interviewer must be prepared for, and aware of, what is occurring during this portion of the inquiry. This was a very important indication of the subject's guilt and, in this particular case, the interviewer didn't catch it.

3. Lying brings anxiety and guilt feelings. Even a deceptive person will try to remain technically truthful while still being deceptive.

A broker was being interviewed regarding an insurance transaction. He was contending that he was totally unaware of another broker's involvement with the same client. The interviewer took the following tact in approaching the subject.

Interviewer: "It was my understanding that ABC Brokerage mailed you copies of all of their correspondence. Are you saying that you didn't receive them?"

Subject: "They didn't mail us anything!"

Note that the interviewer specifically used the verb, "mailed", in the sentence preceding the question. Yet, the question itself was not specific. It asked only whether or not the subject received the copies. The subject chose to utilize the verb, "mail", in his denial, having taken that verb from the sentence preceding the question. It is interesting that he felt the need to be specific in the transmittal verbiage in his response. If he had not received anything, why restate the verb, "mail"? Why not just say, "We never received anything?"

In this particular case, the subject had received the copies by facsimile transmission, and the interviewer knew it. He only used the verb, "mailed", in an effort to bait the subject. This allowed the subject to choose how he would make his denial. By grabbing onto and using the verb provided, he handed the interviewer an important clue to the possibility that he was being deceptive. The interviewer followed up this response.

Interviewer: "How about fax? Did they fax you anything?"

This prompted the subject to become a study in non-verbal behavior activity as he groped for a way to respond. Ultimately, an admission followed.

By being aware that the subject will make an effort to remain truthful in a very technical sense, we, as interviewers, may use that knowledge to our advantage. As in this case, we may alter our questioning tactics in order to enable us to bait and trap the deceptive subject through the way in which we phrase our questions.

4. **The interviewer must never use words or language that the subject has not used first.**

Throughout the interview the interviewer is constantly working to solve the subject's linguistic code. What a word means to one person is not necessarily the same as what it means to someone else. It is important that the interviewer refrain from introducing any new vocabulary to the interview. He has had, after all, the advantage of listening to the subject's narrative of the story and is thus armed with a large array of the subject's words to utilize. The interviewer should stay within the range of words already utilized by the subject when formulating his questions.

If the subject, for example, has not used his wife's name during the interview and only referred to her as his wife, the interviewer must not use the name either. What would be important for the interviewer to learn is at what point the subject changes and begins to use his wife's name. What is the context of the point where this change occurs? What, if anything, does it mean? Can we learn something more about his relationship with his wife through the change in his language?

A man talking about going to several doctors for treatment of his disability, constantly referred to them all as "Quacks!" Later in the interview, the subject called a different doctor a "physician". This change in the subject's language indicated to the interviewer that the subject held this particular doctor in a higher esteem than the others. Why? This could be an important clue in the interviewer's evaluation of the subject's medical treatment.

5. A question must never begin with negative expectations attached.

As stated earlier, people are not afraid to answer questions. They are only afraid to ask them. It is a natural human tendency to fear confrontation by asking sensitive and personal questions. This may cause even some of the most stout of interviewers to give pause on occasion. This does not mean that the interviewer will refrain from asking the question, but he may try to soften it to prevent an emotional response from the subject. This can be a very critical mistake.

A claimant to a life insurance policy was interviewed regarding the death of her husband, who was murdered. The investigator, sensing a perceived frailty in the woman, asked the question in this way.

Interviewer: "I know this may be difficult for you to talk about, but can you tell me what happened the night your husband was killed?"

What's wrong with this? What has the interviewer just told the subject? What will happen the first time the subject is asked a difficult question? What will the subject say then?

Subject: "I'm sorry. This is too difficult for me to talk about."

Clearly, this approach has just handed complete control of the amount of information imparted directly to the subject. The subject need only invoke the magic words given to her as her escape clause and say, "This is too difficult to talk about." The interviewer has already assured her that he will accept that clause and cease questioning on whatever point at which she chooses to invoke it. By beginning the question with the negative expectation, the interviewer has assured himself that he will not obtain all of the information. Since this was a murder case and the wife had not yet been ruled out as a suspect, the interviewer has also prevented himself from working with any direct or confrontational questions. The subject, after all, already knows that the interviewer fears the emotional response and she will use it to control him. All of this comes from the issuance of a negative expectation to preface the question.

Every interview must be approached with the expectation to obtain all possible information and nothing less. The interviewer must repeatedly demonstrate his dogged determination to learn the truth, regardless of obstacles. We know that as long as the subject feels an expectation to talk, he will talk. As interviewers, we need only stay out of the way and let it happen.

6. Questions must never be leading or multiple choice.

In order to ascertain that we obtain the full truth, we need to keep the free flow of choices of response fully within the subject. No question should ever predict, dictate, or restrict a response.

In an automobile accident personal injury case, the subject was questioned about the doctors from whom he had sought treatment. The interviewer was attempting to document as much information as possible about the subject's activities in this area.

Interviewer: "Who did you see first, Dr. Smith or Dr. Jones?"

This question has just eliminated every other doctor on the planet. The subject, if he wishes to conceal any of his medical efforts, need not come forward with the names of any other doctors. The interviewer has just told the subject which doctors he was aware of and granted him freedom from adding any additional names. In this way, the interviewer has completely restricted the information that he will be able to obtain in this interview.

A subject being questioned regarding his activities on the evening of a convenience store robbery was asked his whereabouts. It was the intention of the interviewer to ascertain whether or not he had been in the area of the robbery.

Interviewer: "Were you at the bowling alley or were you still at work at 8:00 P.M.?"

This question has just eliminated all other possibilities for the subject and has enabled the subject to have a window into the limited knowledge of the interviewer. He now knows that that the interviewer did not have any proof or knowledge of any other locations where he may have been. Armed with this, the subject now controls the direction of the interview.

Even though we have entered into the Detailed Inquiry portion of the interview process, it is still incumbent upon us, as interviewers, to continually force the subject to make choices concerning what to tell us. As interviewers in our search for truth, we must be mindful that our goal is to elicit the information in its purest form. As such, it is essential to remain impartial in the process and remember that each word which we speak has the propensity to contaminate the response.

PART 4

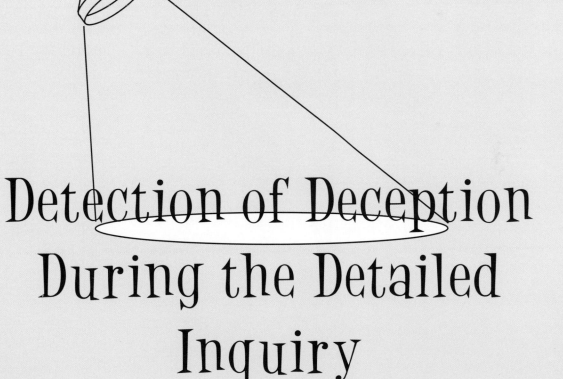

Detection of Deception During the Detailed Inquiry

CHAPTER XXIV

Defeating Resistance

There are two ways in which a subject may resist imparting information. He may do this through either the direct content or the structure of his response. If a subject says, "I will not talk to you!", there is little the interviewer can do. He can try to dissuade the subject from this stance by reasoning with him or questioning his motives for refusing to participate, but he can do little more. If the subject stands firm and will not speak, then the interview is over. The more subtle and common way for a subject to resist can be found in the format which he chooses to utilize while responding to the interviewer's questions.

In the beginning of the interview we set about to take immediate control through the use of Personal Data Questions. This method dictates the roles of the interviewer and the subject. The interviewer's sentences all end with a question mark (?). The subject's sentences all end in a period (.). The flow of information is moving in only one direction.

As we go through the interview, what do we do if this pattern is disrupted? How should the interviewer handle a subject's resistance to the process when it takes the form of the subject questioning the interviewer?

Interviewer: "Where did you go when you left the restaurant?"

Subject: "Why do you need to know?"

What just happened here? The subject broke the pattern. Instead of answering the question, he has brought up a roadblock which prevents the interviewer from exploring this particular area. The subject could have a host of reasons for doing this. He may feel that this information is personal, confidential, and not pertinent to this interview. He may have something to hide that is relevant to the reason the interview is being conducted. He may be attempting to wrest control away from the interviewer before getting to a point which he wishes to conceal. There could be many, many reasons for it. Whatever the reason, the subject IS resisting and blocking the process.

How do we handle this type of resistance? The first thing to consider is the ramifications that would occur if the interviewer were to actually answer the question.

Interviewer: "Where did you go when you left the restaurant?"

Subject: "Why do you need to know?"

Interviewer: "I'm investigating an incident in your neighborhood that happened last night and I need to establish where you were and what you did."

Subject: "What happened? Why do you want to focus on me? Do you intend to talk to anyone else about this?"

It's easy to see the result. The subject is now in charge and the interviewer has become the interviewee. Even of greater concern is that the subject has successfully blocked the interviewer from exploring his activities from the point that he put up the roadblock. The interviewer may regain control later, but significant damage has been done. The subject has bought time to think of the best answer and he has forced the interviewer to reveal the direction of the inquiry, thus enabling himself to better prepare for other questions.

There are two tactics that the interviewer can employ when faced with this type of resistance.

THE DIFFICULT QUESTION TACTIC

This is a simple technique that merely meets a question from the subject with a new question from the interviewer.

Interviewer: "Where did you go when you left the restaurant?"

Subject: "Why do you need to know?"

Interviewer: "Why is this difficult for you to answer?"

Subject: "It isn't!"

Interviewer: "Okay, so where did you go when you left the restaurant?"

In this way, the interviewer has revealed no new information to the subject, broken the roadblock, and maintained control and direction of the interview. Other ways this same approach could be expressed include:

1. "Did you not understand the question?"

2. "Is there a problem with this part of your story?"

3. "Is there something you don't wish me to know?"

4. "Did something happen that you're worried about?"

5. "Are you afraid to answer or to tell me any more?"

While this tactic works very well, there is another useful method that can be employed to beat this type of obstruction.

THE REPEATING TACTIC

This technique is based on the fact that human beings are limited in their bank of negative responses. It is difficult to say, "No". By not answering a question, a person is, in fact, saying, "No". This creates internal guilt feelings and they are compounded when repeated.

As interviewers, we can capitalize on this phenomenon by utilizing this knowledge and simply repeating the question exactly as it was asked the first time.

Interviewer: "Where did you go when you left the restaurant?"

Subject: "Why do you need to know?"

Interviewer: "Where did you go when you left the restaurant?"

Here, the interviewer merely repeats the question, word for word, using the same tone of voice, pace of speech, and style as he had prior to the subject's blocking question. As stated earlier in this book, studies have shown that 97% of the time a person will answer a question the second time it is asked. All the interviewer has to do is repeat the question as if the subject had never spoken.

Utilizing this technique, the interviewer will easily defeat the subject's blocking tactic and maintain the flow of the interview. What if it fails to work? Repeat the question again!

Interviewer: "Where did you go when you left the restaurant?"

Subject: "Why do you need to know?"

Interviewer: "Where did you go when you left the restaurant?"

Subject: "Wait a minute! You didn't answer my question! What concern is it of yours what I did? Why do you need to know? What does it matter?"

Interviewer: "Where did you go when you left the restaurant?"

The subject's ability to resist answering becomes ever more seriously impaired as the interviewer continues to repeat the question. It is important to use the same wording, tone of voice, etc., as were used the first two times. For the subject, the question will begin to sound like a recording being played over and over. This is confusing to him as his objections are ignored and the interviewer stays the course.

Ultimately, the subject will answer the question! In some interviews this pattern has been repeated as many as six times before the subject finally gave in and answered. It should be remembered here that the interviewer holds all the cards. He knows what he is doing. The subject does not. Just as in the case of **Controlled Silence,** the interviewer need only wait it out.

Whether the **Difficult Question Tactic** or the **Repeating Tactic** are employed by the interviewer, they both work to the same end. Each is a method for defeating resistance from the subject and thereby maximizing the amount of data received while detecting deception and/or missing information.

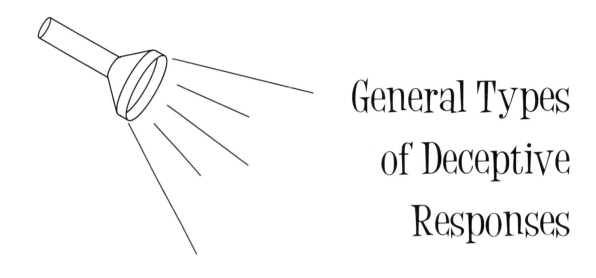

CHAPTER XXV

General Types of Deceptive Responses

As we work through detailing the information in an inquiry, we analyze the subject's responses very carefully, looking for clues to deception, and/or missing information. Some forms of deceptive responses present themselves in a familiar way and are somewhat easy to spot. Let's look at some general types of **Deceptive Responses.**

1. **Qualifies answers**
   The answer is partially restricted in scope.

2. **Calms down quickly after demonstration of anger**
   Truly angry people DO NOT calm down quickly. When this occurs,

it is quite likely that the anger was a tactic utilized by the subject to stall or control the interview at a critical point.

3. **Needs time to "think" of the best answer.**
   This hesitation may be accompanied by a comment such as, "Wait a minute, let me think!"

4. **Seeks information from you about what you know**
   The deceptive subject's answers are often hinged upon learning how

much the interviewer already knows, so that the answer may be adjusted to accommodate.

5. Liars lie specifically

A deceptive subject may choose to be very specific in his answers in order to remain technically truthful, while still continuing deception. "I didn't go there Saturday!", does not exclude any other time. "I didn't file a claim with John Doe Insurance Company!" does not deny a claim with any other company.

CHAPTER XXVI

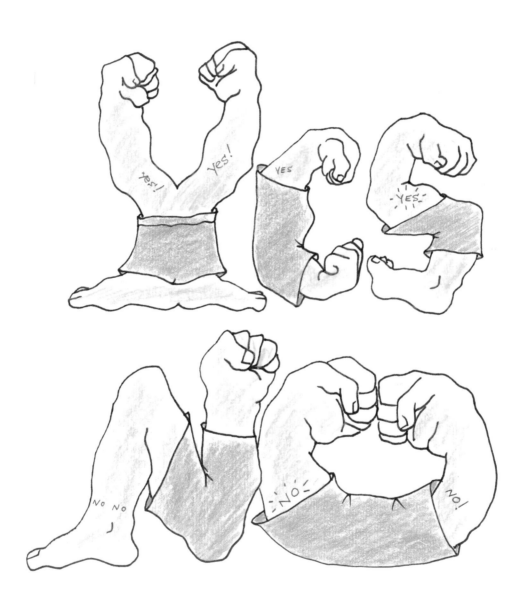

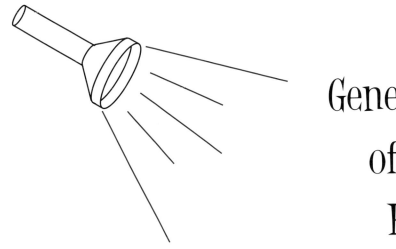

General Types of Truthful Responses

While deceptive responses may often take a common recognizable form, truthful responses may do so as well. It is equally important to identify the truthful subject as well as the deceptive one. Let's look at some general types of **Truthful Responses.**

1. **Strong "Yes" or "No"**
   This could be manifested in voice tone or volume, physical movement, etc.

2. **Willing to be emphatic**

3. **Needs time to calm down after being angry**
   True anger does not dissipate quickly.

4. **Does not need time to "think" of the right answer**
   Response is quick and without hesitation.

5. **Uses minimal information to make a point**

6. **Tells you what you want to know, requires minimal questioning**
   Displays an eagerness to help you resolve your questions.

7. **Truthful persons speak easily and in general terms**

CHAPTER XXVII

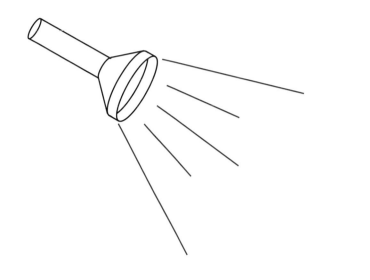

The Word "NO"

The word, "NO", is fascinating. There are many ways to say the word, and yet there are also many ways to interpret it upon hearing it. Since the word, and the message that it carries, are directly associated with guilt feelings and anxiety, the way it manifests itself can be quite enlightening. Here we will examine various ways in which the word may be dispensed.

1. The Five Second "NO"
   This is the person who stretches out the vowel sound in an effort to dramatically increase the effect of the word. It will come out, "Nooooooooooooooooo!" It should also bring concern to the interviewer.

2. The Late "NO" when other responses have been on time

This person is moving along with quick responses until he hits a question with which he is uncomfortable. Hesitation follows, indicating that too much thought is being applied to a simple response.

3. "NO" given too soon, often before the question is finished

This will come about as a result of nervous anticipation or fear of a specific question.

4. The Breathless "NO"

When a question surprises the subject or arrives too quickly and before it was expected, it may bring a brief shortness of breath. This may also happen if there is an emotional tie to the answer or a sensitivity to the subject.

5. The Hummingbird "NO"

A subject feeling unsure about his response may stretch the word out and change tones as he does so. It comes out as almost a sing-song sound.

6. The "NO" followed by chuckling or laughter

We don't normally expect laughter in a interview and certainly not in response to a mundane question. When it occurs out of context, the question that brought it about should be considered as a sensitive one to the subject.

7. Multiple "NO"s

This is the subject who responds, "No, no, no, no, no, no..." He might accompany this verbal response with a lowering of the head, breaking of eye contact, and a shaking of the head as he says this. Such an over-emphasis on the negative response is a good indication that there may be a problem with the answer.

8. The "NO" that only answers half the question

When the question requires more than one answer, it is notable if the response is singular.

Interviewer: "Mr. Jones said that you were at the office on Saturday and Sunday. Is that true?"

Subject: "I wasn't there on Saturday!"

No matter what form the word "NO" takes, it is important to study the relationship between the way in which it is presented as well as other answers given before and after it. If this demonstrates a CHANGE in the subject's language, then it is especially noteworthy and important to determine why it happened.

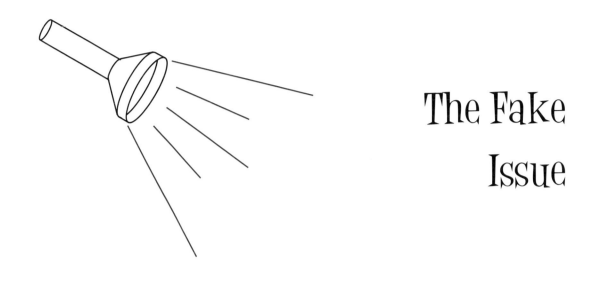

CHAPTER XXVIII

The Fake Issue

One method that a subject may employ in his attempts to stall or control the course of an interview is to bring in the Fake Issue. There are three typical issues that will commonly appear in this strategy.

1. Past Treatment

In this instance, the subject will attempt to bring in stories and examples of how he has been mistreated in the past as a relevant point to what is occurring during this interview. He will attempt to argue that he wouldn't be involved in this interview were it not for prejudicial and preconceived notions about him and therefore this interview is unfair.

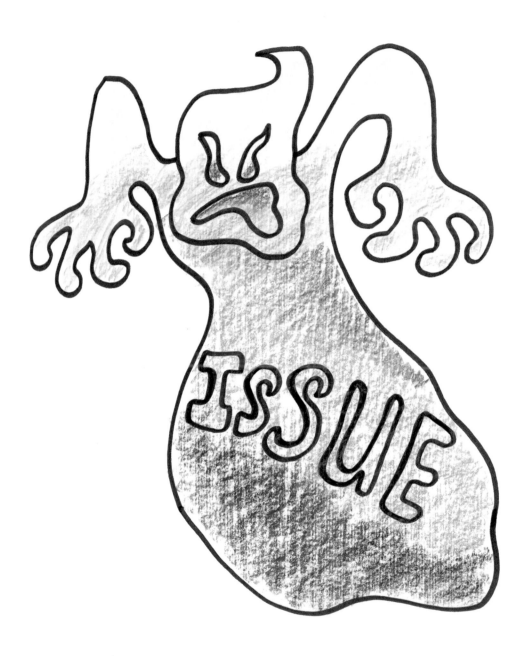

2. Unjustified Anger – over minor questions

Nothing can be more confusing than having a subject react angrily to a minor or insignificant question. The intent of the subject is to bring attention to the trivial matter, thus keeping the focus off the area that concerns him. It also has a secondary function. The subject is attempting to intimidate the interviewer. By bringing confrontation over a minor issue, he is actually hoping to force the interviewer to fear asking him about anything of more importance.

3. Argument over Irrelevant Issues

As in the Unjustified Anger, the intent of the subject here is to derail the focus of the interview. An argument takes time, slows the process, and keeps the spotlight illuminating the wrong area. This is done with an intent to wear down the interviewer as well as to intimidate him.

All of these examples should be regarded as nothing more than blocking tactics and should be treated as such. The best counter to any one of these efforts is an even, factual approach, devoid of personal interest or feeling. Since all of them are intended to bring an emotional reaction from the interviewer, they are best defeated by a stream of cool, calm, unaffected, and undaunted questions.

CHAPTER XXIX

Soft Words

When a person feels guilt or anxiety about a specific event, it is not uncommon to see the use of **Soft Words** employed in an effort to reduce culpability or to diminish the importance of what is being said. These are words that permit the person to tell his story or answer questions in a technically truthful manner while still manipulating the complete truth of the facts.

Let's look at a case of a man being interviewed regarding his activities the night his wife was found murdered.

Interviewer: "What did you and Mary talk about that night?"

Subject: "We had a quiet dinner and neither of us spoke. When we were through, she got up to clear the dishes and we had a **discussion** about her credit card bills."

In this instance, they had actually had a very heated argument. However, the subject was keenly aware of his position as a possible suspect in the crime and therefore was "softening" his description.

Consider the case of a woman who works in a large office, being interviewed regarding missing money.

Interviewer: "Do you know why I've asked to talk with you?"

Subject: "I think it has something to do with some money that was **taken** from a few of the ladies' purses."

Notice the use of the word, "taken", here. The subject is aware that this interviewer was brought in to question workers regarding the missing money. That would certainly imply that there was a theft. Wouldn't we then expect the subject to have used the word, "stolen"? The word, "taken", is a very soft approach to describing what is believed to have happened. Further investigation revealed the reason for this. This subject was the thief. Since she was talking about something that she had done, she had made a verbal attempt to reduce the magnitude of her actions.

A man being considered for an employment opportunity was being asked about an apparent conflict between what he had said during his initial job interview and that which was obtained in the employer's background check.

Interviewer: "You said during your interview that you had never been arrested. We conducted a routine check on your background that indicates that you were charged with embezzlement two years ago while working for Swifto Insurance Company. Why did you omit this information?"

Subject: "That's just a **misunderstanding.** I wasn't really convicted. I never even did any time for that."

In this instance the subject called his lie a misunderstanding. Clearly this is a softer word. The truth is, he lied!

Soft Words can be a very helpful clue to the interviewer. Their presence is a clear indication of sensitivity on the part of the subject and an intention to mask a portion of the truth of what he is saying. This may be turned into an advantage for the interviewer. He may utilize his awareness of the subject's soft words as he plots and formulates new questions.

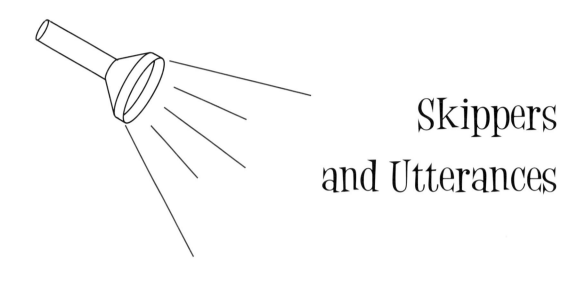

CHAPTER XXX

Skippers and Utterances

Verbal behavior analysis involves more than just the words which a person speaks. **Vocal Skippers** and **Verbal Utterances** can be very meaningful during the interview process. As is true with all forms of verbal and non-verbal analysis, the significance is based upon a notable change in behavior. Does the subject speak freely and easily, for example, and then suddenly initiate a vocal skipping? Is the subject's answer to a question punctuated at the end by an utterance?

Vocal Skippers occur when the subject's speech pattern is disrupted. This will usually be brought on by heightened anxiety, nervousness, fear, etc. The words are accompanied by an unintentional skipper that could be manifested in any of these.

1. Stammering

2. Stuttering

3. Slurring Words

4. Hesitation

Verbal Utterances are a different form of response that are presented in an absence of words. Like the skippers, they are the result of some form of internal pressure within the subject, such as fear, anxiety, worry, etc. These utterances can be representative of the subject's emotional state at the point where they appear.

1. **Whew!**
   This is a sign of relief! The subject is glad to be past this particular point in the interview. It does not necessarily indicate deception. Concern should come if the, "Whew!", occurs at the end of the interview. The subject could be expressing relief that he got through the interview with his deception undetected.

2. **Tisk**
   This is simply an expression of disgust.

3. **Sigh**
   Sighs usually appear as a sign of self-pity. They may represent concession or emotional collapse. If the interview were to be moving into an interrogation, this would be a good sign that the subject was ready.

4. **Nervous Laugh**
   The chuckle or nervous laugh will most times be an indication of fear. Something that is occurring at that point in the interview is extremely uncomfortable for the subject.

Skippers and **Utterances** play an important role in evaluating the subject's state of mind during the interview. Additionally, they give the interviewer an opportunity to alter questioning tactics and direction.

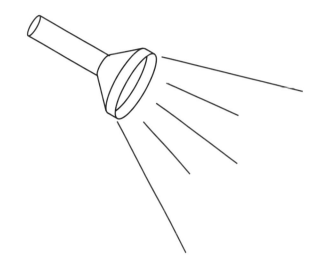

CHAPTER XXXI

Memory Lapses

Memory lapses are an obstacle and a challenge for any interviewer. When encountering them, it is essential to diagnose which form is being presented in order to know how to proceed. While we must acknowledge that there are times when a person honestly doesn't remember something, it does not occur with frequency when we are talking about recent events. If the subject found the event to be insignificant to him when it occurred, he truly may not be able to remember specific details. Similarly, when a person is not focused or interested in what another person is talking about, he may not "hear" what the other person actually said and therefore he would have no real memory of the words. However, when being interviewed about a specific event, the subject of the interview will rarely have been an uninterested party and should usually have memory of it. When there is no memory, we must consider this failure. Simplistically, there are three basic kinds of memory failure.

1. **Blackout**
   This is a physical condition that can occur after severe injury or emotional trauma. We rarely deal with this type of subject, but questioning someone in this state is likely to be quite unproductive.

2. **Repressive Memory Failure**
   This can be brought about by an inability of the subject to face up to the truth of what has happened to him. It can be caused by severe emotional trauma. This person has genuine difficulty accessing portions of his memory. His resistance is not intentional. He is simply emotionally blocked from accepting the facts of a specific event. This type of memory failure will generally surround facts that deal with one specific event or revolve around one specific person. It will not be present at numerous junctures throughout the interview that are not connected.

3. **Motivated Memory Failure**
   It is Motivated Memory Failure that we, as interviewers, are most often presented with. This type of memory loss is the direct result of an intentional effort by the subject to conceal parts of his story or a portion of the facts.

   Let's look at some common indicators that tell us that the subject is experiencing motivated memory failure.

   A. "I don't think so..."
   B. "I can't recall..."
   C. "I can't remember..."
   D. "Not that I can think of..."
   E. "Not that I can remember..."

When a subject is attempting to deceive or to actively manipulate the facts, it is very likely that it will take a form similar to those presented above. These should clue the interviewer in to expand questioning of the events or circumstances surrounding these phrases.

All forms of memory failure can be derailing to an interview. But it is **Motivated Memory Failure** that the interviewer must be keenly aware of and prepared to defeat. The best approach when faced with a subject expressing memory loss is to take the subject back to his last strong memory and move him forward in very small steps through the event.

Interviewer: "When you arrived at the party, was John already there?"

Subject: "I can't recall..."

Interviewer: "Okay, let's go back to your arrival. You said that you rode over there with Bill in his car. It was just the two of you and he was driving. Where did he park the car?"

Subject: "There were a lot of cars there and he had to park a block away and we walked from there."

Interviewer: "Who did you see as you walked toward the house?"

Subject: "There were a lot of people outside of the house, but we didn't know any of them."

Interviewer: "When you entered the house, who did you first see?"

Subject: "Well, Tim let us in, and then after that the only ones there that we knew were Ashley, Mary, Phil, and Suzette."

Interviewer: "What about John?"

Subject: "I don't know..., I can't recall..., was he there yet?"

In this example, the subject was clearly experiencing **Motivated Memory Failure.** By detailing events with him, the interviewer was able to elicit a contradiction which caused the subject to stumble and the result was obvious. Detailing is the best approach to breaking down a motivated memory failure. At times, the interviewer may have to break the steps down into extremely minute parts in order to break the subject's control block. Patience is the virtue here and is key to defeating a subject's **Motivated Memory Failure.**

CHAPTER XXXII

Guilt Signatures

Through the course of the Detailed Inquiry, the subject may present a **Guilt Signature.** This is a response tactic which the subject may employ in order to draw attention away from the his current predicament and the issue at hand. He may do this in a number of ways. Although these indicators should not be considered as conclusive proof of guilt, they do merit notice by the interviewer. Note that they are important only if they occur standing alone and not in reply to an accusation of deception. Let's look at a few examples.

1. Talks about past trouble
This is the subject who begins to relate things that have happened to him in the past where he felt that he was being victimized by others.

2. Admission of something he did wrong in the past that was similar

In an effort to promote his honesty and credibility, the subject may bring up an incident from the past and take responsibility for having done something wrong that was quite similar to the issue about which he is being questioned at this time. His intent is to convince the interviewer that he is capable of admitting this type of thing, but cannot do so in this case because he didn't do it. This tactic is not generally utilized by an innocent person.

3. Speaking in the third person

This may occur when the subject is attempting to put some distance between himself and the issue. By referring to himself in the third person, he actually becomes a different person, acting as a separate entity from the subject being questioned.

4. Accepts that they "look guilty"

Innocent people do not believe that they "look guilty". There may be instances in which an innocent person may reasonably understand their guilty appearance do to certain circumstances or events. However, this will rarely happen if it is not in response to a direct accusation. A truthful subject speaking freely will rarely accept an appearance of guilt, no matter what the reason, unless an actual accusation has been made.

5. Strong denials to virtually everything

This is the subject who is attempting to program himself to be deceptive from start to finish. This subject is attempting to establish a pattern of denial with the hope that it will prevent the interviewer from breaking through it.

6. Accuse the interviewer of prejudice against them

Sometimes the subject will try to divert the issue by going on the offensive against the interviewer. This is accomplished by painting the interviewer as having a prejudicial viewpoint against them and of having a predetermination of their guilt. This prejudice is depicted as purely personal and is not necessarily based upon race, religion, station in life, etc., although any one of these may also be raised.

When a **Guilt Signature** begins to develop, the interviewer must disable it. This may be accomplished by directing questions that force the subject into specifics. It will not be productive to allow the subject to expand on the theme. The faster the interviewer brings the subject back to the process, the more effective he will be in diffusing the tactic.

CHAPTER XXXIII

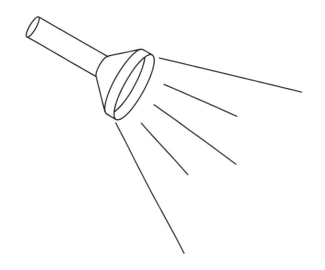

Religious Oaths and Statements

When assessing the information that we acquire in an interview we must continually be cognizant of interpreting the linguistic code used by the subject. Some people will often draw upon religious attachments during the interview as a religion may play an important role in their lives. Others make religious references out of habit or because they were raised by, or spent time with, people who bring religious attachments into things they say.

When considering the significance of the **Religious Oath** or **Religious Statement,** it is important to note its appearance only if it represents a CHANGE in language for the subject. If he continually makes religious

references, then they should be ignored. If there has been no usage of religious references throughout the interview and one suddenly appears, however, then the interviewer must consider it to be important. In this particular instance, the **Religious Oath** or **Religious Statement** will likely mean that deception or, at the very least, extreme sensitivity is present. The following are examples of some of the more common religious references that may appear.

1. **"Honest to God..."**

2. **"If there is a Creator in Heaven..."**

3. **"As God is my witness..."**
   (A favorite response to this one is, "Where should we serve the subpoena?")

4. **"A God fearing person like myself..."**

5. **"I swear on my Mother's grave..."**

6. **"May my parents drop dead if I'm lying..."**
   (This one may lose some effect depending on the subject's relationship with his parents.)

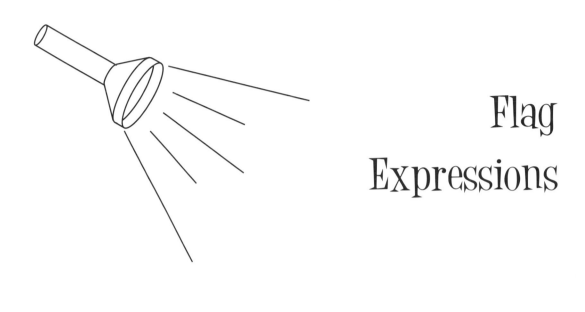

CHAPTER XXXIV

Flag Expressions

Throughout the course of the Detailed Inquiry there are always moments which define the subject's thought processes and direction. These are the comments, actions, remarks, or expressions that we search for as we analyze each response. At one time or another a deceptive subject may err and open a large window into his mind that reveals his concern with detection. These are **Flag Expressions,** general indicators of the presence of deception on the part of the subject. The amount of analytical weight that the interviewer assigns to the emergence of a **Flag Expression** should be based on other supporting evidence. Taken alone, they are not definitive. However, they are excellent guideposts to lead us toward the truth. Let's take a look at some of the more common ones we may hear.

1. "You may not believe anything else I've told you, but you must believe this!"
(Why is that?)

2. "I know you think I'm lying, but..."

3. "I'm not trying to evade the question, but..."

4. "I don't want to confuse you, but..."

5. "You may not believe this, but..."

6. "To tell you the truth..."
(This is a relatively common expression. However, if it has not been used earlier in the interview, then suddenly shows up, beware of the lie that may follow!)

7. "To answer that completely..."

8. "Well, frankly..."

9. "I know this sounds strange, but..."

10. "You're going to find this hard to believe, but..."

11. "I couldn't lie to you..."
(A follow to this might be, "Why not?")

12. "This is going to sound like a lie, but..."
(There's probably a good reason for that!)

13. "To be honest..."
(As in, "To tell you the truth...", this one could be a harbinger of a lie that is to follow.)

14. **"Honestly..."**

15. **"I have absolutely no reason to lie..."**
    (People who are not lying do not talk about reasons to lie.)

16. **"To clarify what I've been saying..."**

17. **"I'm not that type of person..."**
    (A follow to this might be, "What type of person are you?")

CHAPTER XXXV

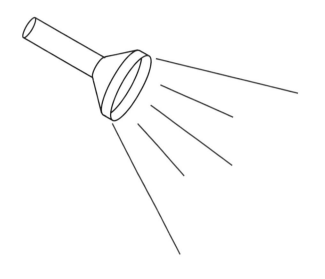

Deceptive Referral

As we have learned, lying begets anxiety and guilt feelings. It is generally difficult for a person to directly tell a lie. That is the basis for the changes in language which we observe as we seek to analyze verbal behavior in a statement or during an interview.

This phenomenon may also evince itself by way of **Deceptive Referral.** This happens when a subject is asked a question to which he has already responded with a direct lie. Rather than repeat the lie and bring forth the accompanying anxiety, the subject will instead refer to the earlier lie. This makes the referral itself a technically truthful statement and therefore much more comfortable to state. Let's look at an example.

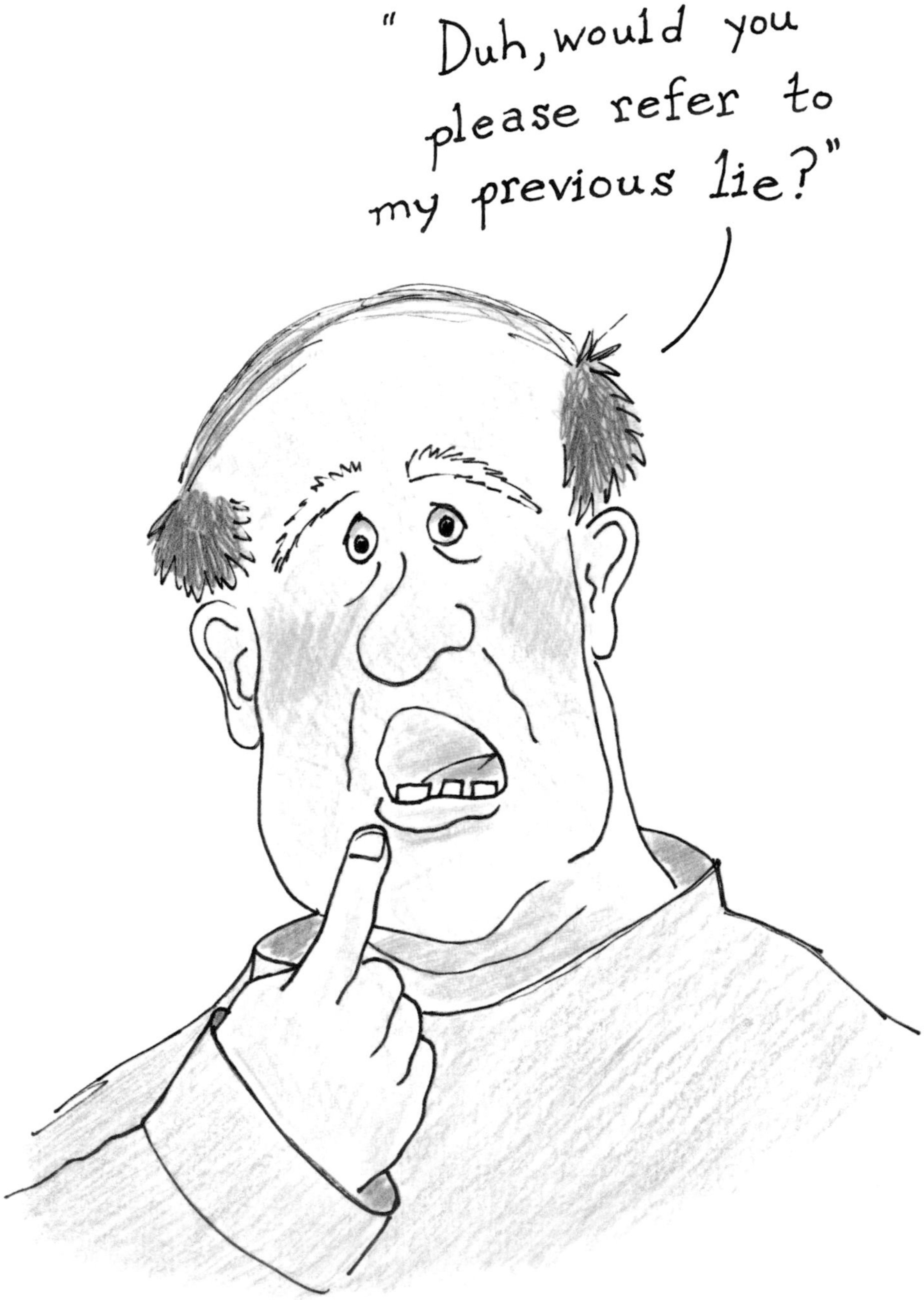
" Duh, would you please refer to my previous lie?"

Interviewer: "Were you inside the store when the shot was fired?"

Subject: "No. I was in my car out front."

Later on in the interview...

Interviewer: "Did you see Tom shoot the clerk?"

Subject: "I already told you, I was in the car!"

In this case, the subject had witnessed the shooting. When the interviewer asked him if he had been in the store at the time, the subject issued a direct lie, stating that he had been in his car.

As the interview wore on, another question came to the subject regarding his whereabouts, and this time it was more closely related to the issue at hand. Rather than repeating the direct lie, which would then have created even greater anxiety, the subject lessened his discomfort by simply referring to the previous lie.

The statement, "I already told you, I was in the car!", was a truthful one. That is, in fact, what he had said earlier. It was not, however, a new denial. It was only a referral to the previous one and should be recognized as such. The subject's hesitancy to repeat his denial may be noteworthy.

In another case, a woman was questioned by an investigator about a credit card theft which had occurred in her office. It had been determined that the time of the theft had been around one o'clock in the afternoon.

Interviewer: "Where were you around one o'clock in the afternoon last Thursday?"

Subject: "Like I told my boss yesterday, I was down in the cafeteria having lunch at that time."

The interviewer was aware that the office workers had all been questioned by the management staff the day before. That knowledge made this response stand out as a possible clue regarding the truth of the subject's answer. Why did the subject begin by stating, "Like I told my boss yesterday..."? All she really needed to say was, "I was down in the cafeteria having lunch at that time." She didn't need the first phrase.

If the subject did tell her boss the day before that she had been in the cafeteria at the time of the theft, then the statement made to the interviewer would be a truthful one, regardless of whether or not she had been in the cafeteria. She was doing nothing more with this answer than telling the interviewer what she had told her boss the day before. She was not attesting to the truth of what she had said, only that it WAS said. If the original response had been a lie, then she successfully avoided eliciting the same guilt or anxiety that she would have experienced had she repeated the lie.

A referral of this type does not necessarily mean that it is a deceptive response. It is only an indicator that should make the interviewer more sensitive to the piece of information involved. Being aware of **Deceptive Referral** is just another tool to be utilized when sorting out the truth of the information which we receive.

CHAPTER XXXVI

Repeats

Sometimes during the course of detailing the information, we will encounter **Repeats.** These are practices employed by the subject as stalling and blocking tactics. The purpose may be to slow down the pace of the interview in order to allow the subject to think about his answer, or it may be to completely block the interviewer from pursuing a particular direction which concerns the subject. In either case, the point under discussion when a **Repeat** appears is usually a critical one in the mind of the subject. Repeats will usually be presented in one of four ways.

1. **The subject asks the interviewer to repeat the question.**
   When the subject goes along answering question after question

without difficulty before suddenly stopping and asking to have the question repeated, it must be noted. Why, we must ask, did the subject suddenly become unable to hear or understand the interviewer's question? This would represent a CHANGE in the subject's own language pattern and, therefore, be quite critical to the analysis of truthfulness.

2. **The subject repeats the question before answering it.**
Much like asking the interviewer to repeat, the subject who repeats the question himself is seeking to buy time to think about his answer. Again, this is important only if it represents a change in the subject's language. Then, if it occurs, it is extremely noteworthy.

3. **The subject says, "I've already answered that question."**
This is akin to the Deceptive Referral discussed previously. It differs only in its intent. Here, the subject is attempting to deflect the question altogether and thus obstruct and redirect the interviewer's direction on the inquiry.

4. **The subject says, "Like I told you before...".**
This may be a form of Deceptive Referral, though the tactic may also be put to use as a blocking agent.

PART 5

Closing

the Interview

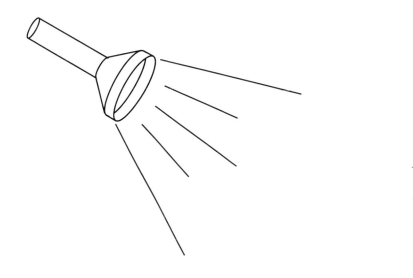

CHAPTER XXXVII

Story Reversal

At the close of the interview, it must be determined whether all of the necessary information has been obtained. It must also be ascertained that that which is true and that which is not true have been effectively sorted out. Despite the interviewer's best efforts, however, uncertainty may remain, leaving him unsure about what has transpired and whether the subject has been truthful.

One method that can be applied in such a situation is **Story Reversal.** This technique is nothing more than asking the subject to retell his story, in reverse order. When a person is relating truth, he is accessing his memory. Every event has a connection to another event, as memory is a finely woven fabric of intricate connections. To recall an event, a truthful person need not start at any particular point in his memory. He can start anywhere and go forward or backward without difficulty.

Conversely, fiction is created in a vacuum. It has no association with real history or fact. It is created in one direction and one direction only. This, therefore, presents a real problem for someone who has fictionalized his account of a series of events. He knows how to start the story and work to the end. What he cannot do is tell it in any other direction without great hesitation. The interviewer may capitalize on this knowledge with this technique. First, however, he must sell the concept to the subject.

A man was suspected of being involved in a hit an run accident. The investigator interviewing the man had asked him to relate everything that had happened on the night in question. At the end of the interview, he went to the **Story Reversal** technique.

Interviewer: "Before we wrap this up today, I want to make sure that I've understood everything you've told me. It has been my experience that if a person goes back over a series of events in reverse order, he sometimes is able to remember certain details that he was previously unable to recall. Since it is very important that we are clear on all of the facts here, I would like you to go over your story again, starting with the last thing you told me and working back to the beginning. Now the last thing you said was that you parked your car in your garage. What happened before that?"

Subject: "I drove home from my girlfriend's house."

Interviewer: "And before that?"

Subject: "Well, I had just dropped her off."

Interviewer: "Go on!"

Subject: "Ah, she and I had just gotten back from a party."

Interviewer: "Continue."

And so on.......................

In this way, the interviewer forces the subject to go through his story step by step. If there is a fictional account mixed in with the facts, it will be very difficult for the subject to do this. He will be forced to hesitate and consider each fact in order to fit it into its original position within the story. The interviewer should limit his questioning to avoid helping the subject to get his bearings. He need only sit back and watch, looking for the point where the subject may alter something he had said previously. At the end of this **Story Reversal,** the interviewer can then bring out and question the contradictions that came up.

Interestingly, if the story was true, this technique can actually help to improve the subject's memory and new and important facts may emerge. Thus, it serves an important purpose whether or not we are dealing with a deceptive subject. It is an excellent device which may help to expand and verify the information obtained during the interview.

SPLIT REVERSAL

A variation on this theme is the **Split Reversal.** Here, the interviewer starts the subject at the middle of the story and takes him back to the beginning. Then, he puts the subject at the end of the story and takes him to the middle. This is even more difficult for the deceptive subject to do and is quite likely to expose the false information.

CHAPTER XXXVIII

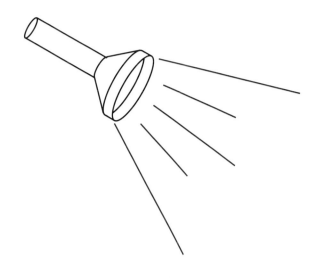

The Line of Deception

Depending on the type of interview being conducted, another mechanism available to the interviewer that may be used in appropriate instances is the **Line of Deception.** This is a very effective approach to judging the overall truth of what was conveyed by the subject during the process.

The **Line of Deception** is a visual aid put into play by the interviewer at the very end of the interview. To do this, the interviewer will hand the subject a blank piece of paper and a pen or pencil. The subject is then in-

structed to draw a straight line on the paper. At one end of the line, he is to write the number "0". At the other, he is to write, "100".

The subject will produce something like this:

0_____100

Next, the subject is instructed to:

Interviewer: "Now, place a mark on this line indicating what percentage of what you just told me was truthful."

Understanding that this technique is not generally employed unless there is a suspicion of existing deception, the resultant effect is still astounding. More than 98% of subjects asked to do this will place a mark at somewhere less than 100%. The most common mark is in the 90's, but some cases have been documented where the subject placed the mark in the middle, indicating around 50%!

Why does this happen? Why would the subject not automatically mark 100%? His goal is to be believed, so why not mark it at the end? What would cause the subject to place his mark anywhere short of the complete truth?

The reason this technique is so effective begins with the basic fact that people try not to lie. That is the basis for the verbal analysis that we have discussed throughout this book. It is difficult enough to lie verbally, but even more difficult to do so in writing. What is being asked of the subject here is for him to certify, in writing, that everything he has said is true.

In addition, the direction itself is assumptive. By telling the subject to place a mark on the line indicating the percentage of what he has said which is truthful, the interviewer has expressed an assumption of the fact that not all of it is. To the subject, the interviewer is telling him that he has already detected some portion of the story to have been deceptive and he is simply asking the subject to tell him how much. The fact that there is deception present has become a given. The subject now feels that he only has control over how much he admits. As a result, he will make a mark less than 100%!

This, of course, opens the interview back up. The interviewer now has an excellent visual aid to work with and may then point to the deceptive portion on the **Line of Deception** indicated by the subject and say:

Interviewer: "Okay, before we close today, let's talk about this part!"

The subject has no choice at this point and will have to admit to something deceptive. In most cases this will lead to other admissions as the interviewer explores the new information.

CHAPTER XXXIX

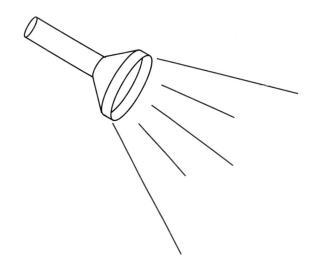

Important Assertions

Information obtained during the interview that is of a meaningful and significant nature must be preserved. Having the subject make the revelation is only half of the battle. The interviewer must then take steps to assure that he does not attempt to change his story in the future. One way to do this is to make the subject repeat the **Important Assertions** at the end of the interview. Statistics tell us that if the subject repeats a statement at least one time, then there is a 97% likelihood that he will never attempt to deny having said it. A best practice is to induce the subject to repeat the **Important Assertions** made during the interview at least three times at its conclusion. Let's examine this approach.

A man being questioned about his involvement in an office theft denied having taken any part in the crime. During the course of the interview, he admitted to driving a coworker to a friend's house with a lap top computer that wasn't hers. The interviewer suspected that it was one of the computers which had been stolen from the business and wanted to lock the subject down on this admission. By doing this, he could identify the coworker as a possible coconspirator at a future time when the computer is recovered.

Interviewer: "Now Ed, you told me earlier that you gave Susan a ride to Mal's house. Isn't that correct?"

Subject: "Yeah, that's right."

Interviewer: "And that was on Tuesday of last week, right?"

Subject: "Yeah."

Interviewer: "And Susan had a lap top computer with her, right?"

Subject: "Yeah, it was a Toshiba."

Interviewer: "And Susan told you she had borrowed it. Is that right?"

Subject: "Un, huh...she doesn't have one of her own."

Interviewer: "When Susan got out of your car at Mal's house, did she take the computer with her?"

Subject: "Sure. What was I supposed to do with it?"

Interviewer: "Now, you said the computer was not in a carrying case, right?

Subject: "Un, huh...I thought that was a little strange. She was just sort of holding it under her arm with a couple of wires hanging down."

And so on.........................

The interviewer in this case took great pains to detail this part of the story at the close of the interview. In this way, he has brought about the subject's psychological commitment to the truth of these facts. By using assumptive questions, the subject was asked only to agree with the interviewer's summary of the facts which had been previously revealed in order to gain his commitment to the truth of them. It also caused the subject to add minor details that cemented the story.

Requiring the subject to repeat the **Important Assertions** at the close of the interview is a great precursor to the obtaining of a written statement. If a statement is appropriate, the best time to request it is immediately upon the completion of this process. Since the subject is now totally committed to the **Important Assertions** which he has made, he has drastically reduced his ability to resist putting the information in writing. With the subject locked in on his account in this way, inducing him to impart a thorough and meaningful written statement is only a short step away.

CHAPTER XL

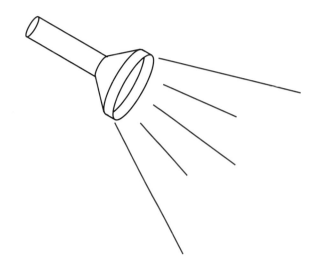

The Exit Strategy

Sometimes, as new information comes to light, it becomes necessary to re-interview a subject in the future. Every interview should be closed with that possibility in mind and with a preparation to initiate it should the eventuality arise. Many interviewers will close with something akin to:

Interviewer: "Okay, thanks for your time today. I think that covers everything. If I need anything else, I'll let you know."

The problem with this approach is that it does not commit the subject to any cooperation in the future. Here the interviewer is only indicating a

possible re-contact without obligating the subject to participate. This can be a fatal mistake.

A preferred method is to bring the subject to agree to future contact and questions. The subject must be forced to make a psychological commitment to cooperate with further inquiries. We can do this by saying:

Interviewer: "Okay, I want to thank you for your time today. If I have any other questions, you would agree to talk with me again, wouldn't you?"

Once again, we see the utilization of the assumptive question, this time assuming cooperation. The subject will now have a difficult time refusing to be questioned again. If he does, we may say:

Interviewer: "I don't understand. When we spoke before, you agreed that you would talk with me again. Why are you now unable to do so? What's changed?"

This brings the subject to feel a need to justify his breaking of the earlier agreement. With the bank of negative responses within a person being limited, the subject's resistance is reduced. Further, having to explain the change at all has already begun the new interview.

Post Script

Every day we learn more in our study of human behavior. As a professional interviewer, it is my responsibility to be steadfast in the search for new and innovative ways to improve upon my techniques and strategies. I may never rest upon past successes or cease in my quest for erudition.

With this book I have endeavored to bring the reader a systematic and analytical approach to the information gathering interview. This methodical process seeks to maximize the amount of information gleaned, identify deception, and detect missing information. It is efficient and effective. It works! It is not, however, all there is to know.

If the reader has found this book to be enlightening, don't stop here. Seek out other theories and practices. Read, listen, and absorb all that you can find. Above all, never be satisfied with what you know. There is always one more little thing out there that could make the difference in a future interview.